# Out the Line

# Out the Line

O. S. NOCK

PAUL ELEK LONDON

First published in Great Britain 1976 by
ELEK BOOKS LIMITED
54-58 Caledonian Road London N1 9RN





ISBN 0 236 40070 3

Printed and bound in Great Britain by
Unwin Brothers Limited
The Gresham Press, Old Woking, Surrey

# Contents

# List of illustrations

*The plates appear between pages 54 and 55*
*Except where otherwise attributed the photographs are the author's*

*Diagram and maps*

# Preface

About twelve years ago when I was up in Inverness doing some research for a book on the Highland Railway, I came across a collection of anecdotes about the trains and the men who ran them under the generic title of *Out the Line*. It was written largely in the vernacular, but in its sketches of personalities and their work, of the old passenger guards, the stationmasters, the drivers and firemen, it breathed the very spirit of the Highland Railway of the late nineteenth century; and when Mr Paul Elek asked me to consider writing a book about my own railway reminiscences the title *Out the Line* seemed to fill the bill more appropriately than something more grammatically correct like *Out on the Line*, or *Work on the Line*, because this is essentially a personal book, rather than something carefully descriptive of a particular operation, machine, or traffic complex. I have written much of this sort, ranging from papers with a professional slant to locomotive and railway history and biographies of famous men.

Railway enthusiasts are always athirst for fine detail, and I shall always remember a critique of one of my books, into which a vast amount of detail had been packed, in a journal of one of the oldest of the enthusiast societies. The reviewer, to my utter amazement at the time, said that the book was 'descriptive rather than factual'! Well, those thirsting for more detail will not find it in this book, I am afraid. It is, instead, a story of some of the adventures I have had 'out the line', in collecting data for some of the many other books I have written, and in carrying out my duties as engineer to a famous firm of railway contractors, which became more diverse as time went on. I have drawn aside the curtain a little to tell how a design engineer, whose work was very much of an 'indoor' nature, came to ride on locomotives in countries all over the world; how what had been an abiding interest from the cradle became the basis of my professional career, and how later my work and my hobbyist railway interests became so intertwined that it was hard to tell sometimes where one stopped and the other began—a situation that was not infrequently turned to the advantage of my employers.

My literary output was at times a matter for speculation. One co-author who also had the pen of a ready writer averred that I must have a team of 'ghosts' devilling for me; and a member of British Railways' staff visiting the Westinghouse works at Chippenham asked to be shown the sanctum where I was secluded, away from all the turmoil of engineering design and production, writing my books! I shall never forget the look on the face of one of my assistants at this suggestion, nor how he said 'I wish we could lock the old Guvnor away sometimes'! This brings me to another point by way of introduction, to express my gratitude: gratitude to men and women, in every walk of life, in many countries, who have been so unstinting in their help. This is not an autobiography, otherwise there would be many other things to tell, and many more people to thank. But there are enough of them in all conscience concerned with the stories I have to tell in this book—those who gave me responsibility in business, and literary opportunities; those who worked with me, and in later years those who worked for me; and those who were just there, and gave me of their advice, and warm friendship. I hope they all realize how grateful I am.

Last, and most important of all, there is Olivia, my wife. As the time of our ruby wedding draws near I realize more and more what it is to a wife, however loving, to have a husband who is rapt up in his profession, and who in his spare moments goes dashing off on numerous extra-mural activities. Even the table talk tended to be 'one track' at times, and I still chuckle over one episode when our son had barely entered into his teens. For some reason the conversation at dinner one night turned upon history, and Olivia said 'I was never very good at that: you know, Cromwell was King in 1245, and that kind of thing!' Our son took it up immediately: 'What did you say, Mummy, Cromwell put a "King" on the 12.45?' As wife and mother, as literary critic, as secretary, as host to my many railway friends, she has excelled.

Silver Cedars,
High Bannerdown,
Batheaston, Bath.

O. S. Nock

May 1976

# 1 The Beginnings, in England

My interest in railways dates from the cradle. From our home in the middle of Reading my mother used to take me in a push-chair to a footbridge at Southcote Junction, where around 1907 I saw some of the West of England expresses of the Great Western using the new short route to the west, via Newbury, Westbury, and Castle Cary. In later years she often told how she got frozen yielding to my appeals to stay on the bridge for just one more train, and how infrequent they were. My rather unfeeling response was to ask why she did not consult a timetable! Then, in due course, toy trains gave place to scale models and I became the proud possessor of a Gauge I Bassett-Lowke model of the GWR 'Atbara' class 4–4–0 No. 3410 *Sydney*.

At school I enjoyed learning mechanics, and in the early 1920s when my engineering studies were in progress some of the railways gave me walking permits to take photographs from the lineside. From the touchline as it were I began very gradually to absorb the atmosphere of 'the line', once rather more dramatically than I had bargained for. In the period of a summer holiday with my parents at Paignton I had a walking permit on the Great Western main line between Exminster and Brent, including the picturesque stretch along the Devon coast beneath the red cliffs of Dawlish and Teignmouth. At the Dawlish end it included several short tunnels, through which one could usually see from end to end. To reach more favourable photographic stances I ventured through some of these tunnels. On a summer Saturday there were many trains, but the bores were usually wide, and there was a walkway on the seaward side quite clear of the tracks. I went through two of them, pausing in the open while two expresses rushed by; and so I came to the third.

It was longer than the rest, and I was anxious to reach the high wall above the sea on the open stretch between this tunnel and the much longer, sharply curved one through the cliffs at the back of the Parson Rock. I had no torch, and once into the darkness of the tunnel I panicked and began to run. With terrifying suddenness I struck something and went sprawling, over a pile of old sleepers that were in the middle of the walkway. My camera and little attaché case containing sandwiches went flying in the darkness. It does not need much imagination to picture how that incident might have ended, had I fallen more awkwardly than I did, broken a limb, and lain across the rails in the middle of that tunnel. But my number was obviously not then up, for I suffered no more than a few bruises and a tear in my trousers. 'Out the line' indeed. In later years I was to go out many times at night, and in tunnels; and I always took a torch!

Photography was the first railway interest that took me 'out the line', the second arose out of it. As a very young schoolboy I read the *Railway Magazine*, and a monthly feature, 'British Locomotive Practice and Performance', was always a centre of attraction, because it was illustrated by many photographs of express trains at speed. As I grew older, and mechanics entered into school lessons, I began to read those articles as well as enjoying the pictures. I read of fast runs, of feats of load haulage, and I came to learn the merits of various types of locomotive known to me hitherto by their colours and the aesthetic features of their external appearance. And as I looked forward to the day when I also would photograph the trains, so equally came the ambition to compile detailed logs of the running. The opportunity came when I began my engineering studies at Imperial College in the autumn of 1921, and I had to make six long-distance journeys each year from my home at Barrow-in-Furness to London. I took careful notes of the time at which we passed the various stations, and from the mileages published in those *Railway Magazine* articles I worked out the average speeds. It was a pastime that positively grew upon one, and I shall never cease to be grateful to the author of those articles, Cecil J. Allen, for the interest he aroused in me. He was writing them when I was in the nursery. I little thought then that one day, nearly *fifty* years later, I should succeed him directly in the authorship, after he had contributed a grand total of 536 articles.

When I took my engineering degree, in 1924, as a small memento my father presented me with a stop watch, and a family holiday at Penzance enabled me to log the Cornish Riviera Express in much greater detail than my earlier efforts. After my postgraduate year at Imperial College I joined the staff of the Westinghouse Brake and Saxby Signal Company, in York Way, overlooking King's Cross station, and with a little more pocket money I made occasional short trips from London, just for the ride; but before then I had learned how vulnerable the pastime of train timing could be. In other forms of railway enthusiasm the devotee can be something of a loner. The photographer is usually alone by the lineside except for the occasional yarn with a friendly platelayer; the historian browses around the branch lines, and what were once called the 'byways of Bradshaw'. On the other hand the timing enthusiast performs in full and close contact with the travelling public; and anyone using not just one but *two* watches, throughout the journey, is inevitably liable to attract attention and comment. I shall recall two incidents—both most embarrassing, although in different ways.

One summer my parents were on holiday at Paignton, and from London I went down to spend the August bank holiday weekend with them. I returned on the Tuesday by an evening train, and was rejoicing at my luck in finding an empty compartment and the prospect of some enjoyable timing when, at Newton Abbot, a crowd of raucous racegoers, homeward bound, crashed into the compartment and at once, at the top of their voices, embarked on a crossfire of acid comment on the day's results. There were nevertheless some sidelong glances at my watches and my notetaking; and as we were nearing Exeter, in a lull in the storm of words, one of them demanded of me 'Well, what is the time, anyway?' And then it started! Why was I taking the time? What was the use of it? How much was I paid for doing it? But in the midst of it all I learned with relief that they had got into the wrong train, and would be getting out at Taunton. Then they started guessing the speed, and guessing quickly turned to betting on it, with myself as the adjudicator! The whole business was conducted at a racecourse level of decibels, and to me the astonishing thing was that they took my speed readings as absolute gospel, and money changed hands freely on the basis of them. But was I glad when the train drew into Taunton, and they poured out as noisily and precipitately as they had barged in at Newton Abbot!

About a year later I was travelling from Leamington Spa to Paddington by the Shakespeare Express, and again was congratulating myself on finding an empty compartment when, at the last minute, in dashed six American ladies. They had been 'doing' the Shakespeare country; the day had been gloriously fine, the sights they had seen had been terrific, and to one and all life was just great. To me, however, concentrating on other things, it was soon evident that we were in for a record run. But from my corner I noticed that amid the torrent of joyous conversation there were again numerous glances towards my stop watch. I began to fear the worst. The blow fell just as we were beginning the climb over the Chiltern Hills. Then the youngest, and certainly not the least attractive, of my fellow travellers leaned across the compartment and said 'Excuse *me*, but what are you doing with that wa-atch?' It was useless to explain that I was just measuring the speed. The whole party joined in, and bombarded me with questions. 'How did I do it?' 'Where are the mileposts?' The stop watch was passed from one to another. They crowded round the window. Amid shrieks of delight they started and stopped the watch. 'Say, Eleanor, you try; I can't see any mileposts at arl.' We were nearing the outer suburbs of London before their questions ceased, and then the youngest, and I repeat not the least attractive, of them summed up the situation with 'Wa-arl, you sure have been ca-ancentratin'!'

Work 'out the line' always needs a good deal of concentration, and one job during my practical training as an engineer with Westinghouse remains a memory for all time. In the fitting shops at Chippenham I worked on interlocking frames of all kinds, learning the laborious but skilled craft of fitting the pieces that made up the intricate jigsaw puzzle by which a signalman was positively prevented from pulling a wrong lever. I helped to build the miniature lever frame for Edgware Road station on the Inner Circle line, and while working with the fitters I found time to absorb a little of the whys and wherefores: why pulling lever 16, for example, had to lock 20, 22 and 23. About a year later, when my training was continuing in the drawing office in London, the chief draughtsman under whom I was then working had a serious illness and was away for several months. He was an expert of experts in the art of interlocking, and just at this very time a job of extraordinary complexity came in. Two years earlier the big Southern Railway terminus of Cannon Sreet had been resignalled to suit the changeover to electric traction. Now interlocking is an art and a philosophy, not a precision job to which there can be one, and only one, solution; and after early experience with the working of the new plant the traffic officers of the Southern felt that if certain changes were made in the interlocking, without of course in any way affecting its integrity, it would save them the occasional *minute* at peak hours.

To this day I do not know how I, still a trainee, came to be chosen to make the drawings for this very complex alteration, but what I do remember most vividly are the moments of exhilaration, anguish and sheer funk that filled the ensuing month. I was thrilled to get the job, for it was real railway work involved with all the intricacies of train movement in a big London station; but the engineer then in charge of mechanical signalling, himself a locking expert, was asked to supervise my work, and he was an awkward man, alternately playing the familiar roles of ingratiating patronizer and bully. In between the kicks and the compliments I learned a lot, but I was glad when the drawings were finished and sent to the works at Chippenham.

Several months went by, and then one day the chief electrical engineer sent for me and said the equipment was ready for installing. A team of four fitters was being sent up from Chippenham and it was expected that the job would take a month, working entirely at nights.

I was to attend from time to time, help in the fitting, and generally gain experience in the work. 'Out the line' indeed. This was it! The senior draughtsman I was assisting in my ordinary daily work was not amused. 'What's going to happen to my b . . . job,' he exclaimed. I soon found, however, that Cannon Street was very far from an ordinary night shift, and another exciting month began.

The fitting of the new interlocking could not be completed piecemeal. Night by night small sections had to be tried in their appointed places, hand fitted where necessary, and then taken out and the original parts restored. Night by night more and more sections were done, until all was ready for the final changeover, which would be done at a weekend. Alterations to locking mean that the part of the station controlled by the levers concerned was temporarily out of action, and even during the night this was often difficult to arrange. We could rarely get 'possession' of any part of that 143-lever assembly until after midnight, when the last of the suburban trains had gone; and the first of the incoming workmen's trains arrived soon after 5 a.m. But it was June, and there was another complication. The Kentish strawberry season was in full swing, and night after night there were specials bringing enormous loads for Covent Garden. We came to hate the very name of strawberries, for the trains would come up about two or three o'clock in the morning, and their routeing would often prevent us working on many levers that we needed free. The Dover Mail was another headache. It came in at 1.20 a.m., and no diversion or delay to that train was permitted.

I was in digs at Notting Hill at the time, and on my nights out I used to cycle down about midnight. It was a delightful sensation to go pedalling down through the West End and the City with hardly any traffic about; and in the morning I used to see the sun rise behind Tower Bridge before pedalling digs-ward again around 6 a.m. There was little we could do after five o'clock. After my nights out I would sleep in the morning, and then go to my normal work in the drawing office at King's Cross in the afternoons. The final night was hectic. There were normally no trains in the station on a Sunday morning, but the Southern Railway engineer arrived soon after breakfast anxious to begin his inspection, and in the solid, methodical way essential in such a task he tested every one of the 143 levers, whether it had been altered or not, and found all was well. I had not been long in the drawing office on Monday morning, however, before I was summoned to the chief's office. 'There's something wrong with that damned locking' he snapped, and went on to tell that one lever was locked when it should not have been, and that the railway people were furious because it was holding up traffic. I began to remind him that the inspector had passed our work, but he simply leapt down my throat, and told me to check the drawings and find out what was wrong. With two colleagues I went through the disputed pieces, and could find nothing wrong. The chief, by then involved in something else, merely said 'Well, go down tonight and see for yourself!'

I shall never forget that night! It was 9 July 1928, and I did not wait for the witching hour before I made for Cannon Street station. When I got there it did not take me a moment to realize that a 'flap' of the first order was in full blast. My heart missed a beat. Surely my locking had not caused all this! When I climbed up into the signal box I learned to my sorrow that there had been a collision at London Bridge earlier that evening; several lines were blocked and some trains were being diverted into Cannon Street. The news of this accident was alarming, because less than a month earlier the new colour-light signalling at London Bridge had been brought into service, controlled by an enormously larger version of the same type of interlocking frame as that at Cannon Street. But the night signalmen, who by that time I knew well, were reassuring from the Westinghouse point of view: 'It looks as though it was the driver's fault—backed out of the platform farther than he should have done.' Liability or not, however, Cannon Street was in a pretty pickle—cluttered up with trains, nerves taut all round, but with the sense of responsibility of the railwayman never more finely displayed.

Our fitters had not arrived when I got there. After the completion of the job on the previous day, they had taken a justifiable rest, and their reporting for duty on the Monday night was only a matter of routine. The leading signalman explained to me the hold-up in the locking that had been experienced, and although we could not yet free the levers for attention, he took off the front cover of the frame, and I saw at once what was wrong. The bevel on one of the locking dogs had not been sufficiently filed. Two minutes work would put it right. When our fitters arrived they had not heard of the accident at London Bridge, and they were as relieved as I was to hear of the likely cause. For our own work, because of the congestion in the station, the late arrival of the Dover Mail, and two more of those wretched strawberry specials (!), it was nearly daylight before we could have possession of the offending lever and free the locking as it was designed to be. I did not rest that morning but went straight into the office. The chief was far more concerned about London Bridge than our own slight contretemps, so quickly rectified at Cannon Street. He questioned me at length, but when I told him what the night signalmen had said, he was much relieved, and just commented 'They would know.' So it eventually proved to be; and so also in one way or another I grew up at Cannon Street.

Although my professional work was at first entirely in signalling, the love of steam locomotives that used to lie deep in the soul of every boy had already ripened into a keen technical interest. I had joined the Institution of Mechanical Engineers as a student while still at Imperial College, and never missed a meeting at which locomotives were to be discussed. I saw and heard great men of the day whose engines I knew: Sir Vincent Raven of the North Eastern, Sir Henry Fowler of the Midland, R. E. L. Maunsell of the Southern; and I met, as fellow students and graduates, men who, as we climbed our respective ladders, became close friends and colleagues. Many of them were youngsters in the locomotive departments of the various British railways, and I enjoyed nothing more than to get them yarning about their own work. Gradually the ambition grew to ride on the footplate, but for many years the opportunity eluded me.

In the early 1930s the great slump prevailed. There was little work for Westinghouse—so little indeed that many of us lived in fear of being discharged. To try and augment my small salary I began writing articles about railways. The great majority of those early efforts earned nothing more than the editor's rejection slip; but one day I took a long shot, and it came off—and in due course I arrived at Euston with an engine pass in my pocket, to collect data for a commissioned article. My first efforts were directed towards the *Railway Magazine*, of which I had been a reader almost from my cradle; but, tempted by an advertisement which, if I remember rightly, was headed 'More Profit from Writing', I took a correspondence course in journalism, and gathered some pretty caustic comments upon my first efforts at writing popular articles. That course eventually taught me two important things: the need for a compelling, arresting opening paragraph and, when I was writing round technical things, to have a plentiful leavening of human interest. While the second of these necessities was essential for the popular press, it was anathema to professional engineers, who regarded it as a waste of valuable space, and quite unnecessary padding. So at first I had to learn to develop two styles, and truth to tell I had little success with either!

The *Railway Magazine* was the first to publish an article of mine, entitled 'Carlisle, a Station of Changes', in its January 1932 issue, and to convince a somewhat reluctant editor of its attractions I had dashed up there on a winter's night to spend a Saturday morning photographing the trains. I must have been very enthusiastic about railways then, because I find on referring to my travelling diary of the period that I went north from Euston at 12.35 a.m. on the Night Scot, and logged the running in detail. The only section over which the record is missing is from Crewe to Preston. Forty-five years later I am wondering how I managed to keep awake! The conditions on arrival could not have been worse. It was cold, windy, and a mixture of sleet and rain was driving in through the open ends of the station all the morning. Steam was blowing all over the place. In desperation I took many photographs, but the majority were hopeless and, by early afternoon, wet and chilled to the bone, even I gave up and caught the 2.42 p.m. express back to St Pancras. I sold the article, embellished by three photographs which clearly showed the climatic conditions of the day: but as for 'more profit from writing' the fee I eventually received barely paid for my frugal meals on that trip, let alone the return fare from London to Carlisle and back—even at 1931 weekend rates!

My first real success, though not exactly so financially, was when I sold one of my correspondence course exercises to the London *Evening News*, and it was published early in 1932 as a mini-feature under the heading of 'Hyde Park's Ghost Trains', over the cryptic initials 'C.K.S.'. I was doing something of a tightrope act at the time as far as my own professional work was concerned. My immediate boss at the time was a difficult man: intensely possessive, and jealous that no vestige of credit or prestige should come out of his department unless directly attributed to him. I felt, and from the experience of a far more senior engineer than myself with some justification, that any attempt to augment my income at that stage would have brought a veto, if nothing worse. So everything except my contributions to the 'little' *Railway Magazine*, which was regarded as a bit of a joke in some professional circles, had to be written under a pen name. At one time I used my second name, Stevens, prefixed by two letters from my surname, CK; other contributions were under the pseudonym of 'Railway Engineer'. The modesty of my success in those early days may be judged from the number of articles other than in the *Railway Magazine* that I had published. From the beginning of 1932 up to Easter 1934 there were just sixteen, and of those four were in our local paper at Watford.

There was another side to my early efforts in journalism. With the enthusiasm generated by that correspondence course I worked hard to try and develop something other than articles with a railway slant, and my love of the country and keenness on purely pictorial landscape photography came to my aid. I found an occasional market in the *Motor*, although while I was a driver I could not afford a car! In accepting my small articles I do not think the editor ever discovered this. Still writing as 'C.K.S.' I had such articles as 'A Lonely Scottish Lido', 'The Gateway of the Lakes' and 'The Country of St Abb', while the *Riley Record* published 'The Lower Eden Valley'.

Almost the last of these, and perhaps in retrospect the best, appeared under my own name in the *Glasgow Herald* in November 1934, 'Autumn in Moidart'. But by that time the more technical side of my authorship was beginning, and such time as I could spare for writing became devoted more and more to railways. I must now tell how I came to take the 'long shot' that opened up a collateral course in my life that has led so far to more than eighty, not articles, but full-length books.

With a few short mini-features I was lucky enough to catch the eye of Wilson Midgley, features editor of the *Star*. Beginning in June 1932 he took 'Signs for the Colour Blind' from me. Then followed 'A Robot Railway', 'Pacific 1933', 'East London's Searchlights', 'Speed Up to Paris'—in the course of about two years. 'Pacific 1933' was his re-titling of a piece on the first Stanier 'Pacifics' of the LMS, which came out that year. I forget what my own title was, but Midgley skilfully parodied the title of Honnegger's well known fantasia 'Pacific 231', which was played recently to excellent effect at the musical night at the Albert Hall, organised by British Railways at the time of the 150th Anniversary of the Stockton and Darlington Railway in 1975. Anyway, right back in March 1934 I wrote to the *Star* and asked if they would like an article describing a footplate ride on 'Pacific 1933'. Midgley did not actually commission an article, but his reply was encouraging enough for me to ask the LMS for the necessary permission, and to my delight they gave it—not only for the 'Pacific', but to ride any other engine, between Euston and Edinburgh, where I was intending to spend the Easter weekend, that year. I was certainly going in at the deep end. Drivers of those days started as cleaners, and had their first rides round the shed yard. Engineering pupils started their footplate experience on light duties; but here was I going to ride the engine of the Royal Scot express, on Special Limit timings, with the train up to maximum load. I was scared stiff, as well as being exhilarated. I remember the odd feeling of showing the guard my pass, changing into my old works 'slop' in his van, and then leaving my luggage with him and walking up to the front end—empty-handed except for my notebook and watches.

The engine was a 'Royal Scot' 4–6–0, No. 6137 *Vesta*, taking the train right through to Carlisle. The driver and fireman, broad Cumbrians who had worked up to London the previous day, could not have made me more welcome. I have often thought since how lucky I was to ride with Billy Charlton and Arthur Baker on my very first trip. More than forty years later, when my footplate mileage, all over the world, is getting near to six figures, I have found that a footplate pass and a love of engines will quickly break down all barriers of language, creed or colour. But as in everything else there are degrees in the welcome one receives; but never have I been more charmingly received than on *Vesta*. It was a good job too, because the 'Royal Scots' were not the most comfortable engines to ride. For some extraordinary reason the tenders were built much narrower than the engines, and when sitting on the seat on the fireman's side—which was awarded to me—one looked back into an airy nothing!

Despite the friendliness of the men there was an odd feeling of isolation in the cab. One was cut off completely from the cosy familiarity of the train. The feeling was still more odd when we started, and the engine began to gather speed. *Vesta* rode like some great lumbering carthorse. There did not seem to be a spring beneath her, and it was a little time before I became sufficiently acclimatized to take in any of the technical details of her going. For some years I had read avidly every detail of engine performance and testing on which I could lay my hands, but Charlton's method of driving did not match up with any of these—or so it appeared to me. Nevertheless my watches told me we were doing very well, taking our fifteen coaches along at splendid express speed. It did not feel like it. I watched the easy nonchalance of Baker as he fired. Once or twice Charlton beckoned me over to his side of the cab to note his adjustment of the controls, and on that bumping, hard-riding engine I staggered across in most undignified fashion. On my way back I wondered if a sudden lurch would send me over the side, or backwards into that airy nothing! But all was well, and at Rugby, with a blackened face and a great singing in my ears, I went back to the train. Eighty-two miles of top class express running was enough for a start.

That start was the first step in the gradual opening of the door to the most fascinating form of railway travel. It could be rough, very dirty, sweltering hot or biting cold; but all that went with the job. There was the spectacle of a great machine, the most live, vivid, near-human machine ever invented by man, in full action; then there was the team work of driver and fireman, never better displayed than sometimes when things were not going smoothly. Then, added to all this, was the joy of seeing the countryside in all its moods, by morning, noon and night, winter and summer alike. I shall always remember a night of snow squalls when we had driven north from Newcastle, and how as we came on to the Forth Bridge at five on a winter's morning, the clouds parted, and the moon shone out, lighting the great girders as we passed underneath. Or again, there was a Saturday afternoon in rural Devon when, from the footplate of the Penzance–Wolverhampton express, I saw the men of Cullompton at cricket; and almost in the shadow of the tall square tower of the lovely village church I saw hit one of the most spectacular sixes I ever remember. All this, and many other incidents to be told later, stemmed from the time I was washing the imprint of *Vesta* from my face and neck.

There remained a long haul ahead of me. The railways granted footplate permits grudgingly, and only when there was a possibility of publicity in the daily newspapers. Writing in the technical press was considered preaching to the converted, and one of my early articles led to quite a fracas behind closed doors, on the LNER. I had been down from King's Cross to Newcastle on a Gresley 'Pacific', and sold an article to the *Star*. W. A. Willox, then Associate Editor of the *Railway Gazette*, was interested in the data I had collected and asked for a short technical article. When he received it he asked whether Gresley had approved it. I explained that my authority to ride on the footplate had been received from the Press Office at King's Cross. This did not satisfy Willox, and he sent a proof to the Chief Mechanical Engineer's office. Gresley himself was away at the time; his assistant O. V. S. Bulleid got hold of it, and stormed into the Assistant General Manager, demanding to know who had given 'this man Nock' a footplate pass. But at that time the Locomotive Running Superintendents were independent officers, and it was from them that my footplate authority had been issued. 'Exit Bulleid—retired hurt'! I may add however that several years later when I was more established and Bulleid was Chief Mechanical Engineer of the Southern Railway, I had much kindly help from him.

Just before World War II I wrote a series of articles for the *Railway Magazine* on 'The Locomotives of Sir Nigel Gresley', based to some extent on the footplate runs I had already made. Edward Marsden, who was head of the Press Office at King's Cross, had been very interested and helpful, and when the first article appeared in February 1941 he took the magazine in to show Gresley, as he told me afterwards with some trepidation, because, he said, 'when the Great Man is not amused, it is best to seek your quickest line of retreat.' But all was well, and the outcome was rather amusing. Gresley rang up John Kay, Managing Editor of the *Railway Gazette* and the *Railway Magazine*, saying 'Who is this man Nock?', and his only complaint was that the article was inadequately illustrated. It was wartime, however, and the publishers were having to economize; but Gresley brushed this explanation to one side, and promptly sent Kay all his private photograph albums. Those articles were afterwards republished to become my very first book, in 1945.

# 2 Farther Afield

It was through my friend Harry Macgregor Pearson that I first ventured 'out the line' in foreign parts. We had been drawn together during our time at Imperial College by a common interest in railways, but after graduation our ways led us professionally far apart. While I joined Westinghouse, his civil engineering work took him for a time to Belgium where he was engaged on the construction of that great war memorial, the Menin Gate. He travelled much in Western Europe, and then returned to join the Great Western Railway, on which, in 1934, he was surveyor and draughtsman in the Divisional Engineer's office at Shrewsbury. This was many years before either of us was married and when his family planned to spend the Whitsun weekend in Paris, he suggested that I joined them, so that he and I could have our fill of railways while the rest of his family did the traditional sights. We reckoned that if we caught the first boat over on the Saturday we could get in one shed visit in the late afternoon, leaving the other three big ones till the Monday, spending Sunday *en famille*. Mac, writing no doubt as from the GWR, organized all the necessary permits, and late on that Saturday afternoon we set out from the Gare du Nord.

It was part of the game that we used nought but public transport in Paris. We could not afford taxis, and I shall never forget my first whiff of the *odeur* of the Metro! But let that pass. We were soon at the La Chapelle depot of the Nord, and after some confusing preliminary exchanges at cross purposes, arising only from language difficulties—all very good natured and accompanied by much hearty laughter—we were allocated a guide, and went out on to the shed. As I have found over and over again in later years, a mutual love of locomotives is an international passport beyond price, and as we walked round and photographed engine after engine their crews stood discreetly alongside, and then blew us kisses, with requests for copies when they moved off the shed. We were visiting the Nord at a very interesting time because they were acquiring engines from the Paris–Orleans, when that company had many steam locomotives redundant as a result of the extension of the electrified system south and south-west of Orleans. It was at La Chapelle that I had my first sight of one of the magnificent Chapelon 'Pacifics', known on the Nord as the 'P.O. Transformations', and transformations from the original engines they were in very truth. Our guide allowed us to climb on to as many engines as we wished, and I was astonished at the very small amount of space provided on the footplates of even the largest engines, in comparison with the deep, roomy cabs of the latest British locomotives. The French cabs were little more than shelters, with no such luxuries as seats on which the driver and fireman could sit down.

Monday brought us some adventures. The steam locomotive running sheds at La Villette, Bercy, and Les Batignolles are not exactly on the normal tourist routes, and the more we got off the usual tracks the harder it was to make people understand where we wanted to go; in fact two young Englishmen walking round some of the less salubrious quarters of Paris, armed with cameras, caused a certain amount of suspicion, until we actually reached the sheds and showed our permits. Then all was smiles, and profuse greetings. The weather was fine, and we both took scores of photographs. There was an astonishing variety of locomotives to be seen in those far-off years, and the freedom we were allowed to climb over as many as we liked was an invaluable preparation for the great adventure I was to embark upon later.

Three years later, greatly daring, I applied for permission to ride the engine of the Golden Arrow from Calais to Paris. It was readily granted, and on a fine July day I climbed aboard one of the big Nord 'Pacifics' at the Gare Maritime for a 60 m.p.h. non-stop run to Paris. The driver and fireman were friendly, though a little curious at first. A burly running inspector who had been sent to accompany me did his best to explain the working of the engine; but, as neither he nor either of the crew had a *word* of English, it was a bit difficult, and the four-cylinder de Glehn compounds of the Nord are not the simplest of locomotives. The driver, Blondel by name, was quite a young man. In France the training of express enginemen was quite different from what it was in Great Britain. They were more technically educated, and reached top-link duties when in the prime of life. On the Nord in particular they always stayed with the one engine, even to the extent of accompanying it into the works when general overhaul was needed. The driver then helped in the repair and servicing of 'his' engine. They became very skilled in the handling of these complicated engines. By the time I rode this magnificent '3-1252' I had become quite a seasoned footplater and, with the engine riding smoothly, I could devote all my attentions to the working, without having to worry about the niceties of hanging on.

We all wore goggles. The Nord used local coal from the pits in the Pas de Calais; it is very dusty and in three hours of running my face and hands were grimed beyond description. Mixed with this dusty coal were briquettes. They were taken from a stack on the front of the tender, cracked in half with a hammer and thrown in by hand. We got away from Calais with tremendous vigour, climbed powerfully over the hills inland from Cap Gris Nez, and then dashed down through Wimereux and the outskirts of Boulogne. This hilly piece of line needed constant adjustment of the controls; but after Étaples we settled down to a spell of fast level running at 72 to 73 m.p.h., and it was time for refreshment. On English engines I had been treated to all sorts of footplate beverages, cold tea, lemon barley water, 'patent' concoctions; but on this great French 'Pacific' purring smoothly along, with a load of huge Pullmans behind us, we toasted the 'Entente Cordiale' in a light red wine!

Because of heavy traffic we had left Calais somewhat behind time, but Driver Blondel was getting it back steadily. Six-and-a-quarter minutes had been regained by Amiens, and we were racing downhill from Saint-Just at nearly 80 m.p.h. when the unexpected happened. There was a whispered conversation between Blondel and Inspector Baudry, looks of concern, and then to my surprise Baudry climbed out of the cab and made his way along the running plate to the front end. We were still running at about 70 m.p.h., and hanging on with one hand he stooped down to peer into that part of the machinery that was between the frames and beneath the large boiler. When he straightened out again he gave us a sign that something was broken. I never ascertained exactly what part it was that had failed, nor how it was they had scented trouble in the first place. But just as an experienced motorist can quickly detect that something is going wrong with his car long before his passengers sense anything, so Blondel and Baudry noticed some irregularity in the steam distribution in the low pressure cylinders, and one of them went out to look.

Whichever it was of the linkage rods in the valve gear, it had not reached the point of breakage, but it was enough for them to decide to cut the low pressure cylinders out of operation. The complications of the de Glehn controls then came into their own, for Blondel was able to isolate them, and work only on the two high pressure cylinders. The result acoustically was extraordinary. Up to now this beautifully balanced engine had been purring along with hardly a sound, but after Creil with only two cylinders being used for all they were worth the exhaust became a roaring tattoo that made every railwayman at the lineside gape with astonishment. The Frenchman is a past master in the making of expressive gestures and our fireman,

Mantez, equally a humorist, exhibited the last degrees of dejection in response to the expressions of the lineside *cheminots*. We should have been doing about 55 m.p.h. up the long incline through Chantilly, but the best we could do, for all the noise the engine was making, was 41 m.p.h. It was mighty good all the same with only half the engine in action.

Our laboured ascent was nothing to what happened when we got over the summit and began the descent towards Paris, for Blondel continued to use those two cylinders to the utmost, and the continuing roar as the speed climbed to 60, 65, and then to 70 m.p.h. was terrific. As the needle of the speedometer crept up to 110 kilometres per hour (68 m.p.h.) Baudry yelled '*Cent dix*', and literally jumped for joy! By the time we got to Paris most of the eight minutes Blondel had regained by Creil had slipped away, and not surprisingly, but we had still bettered the normal end-to-end timing, by doing the 184 miles from Calais in 188¾ minutes. Baudry did his best to show me and explain what had happened; but in the semi-darkness, and between the engine frames, it was difficult to see, as well as to follow his words. In my write-up the incident was thus described in fairly general terms; but when I sent it to Monsieur Lancrenon, the Chief Mechanical Engineer of the Nord, he was kind enough to approve it without alteration.

My troubles began when a more detailed description of this and other French footplate journeys was published in *The Engineer*. Even in professional circles there are always correspondents who delight in trying to show how wrong everyone is except themselves; and there are others who could be described as professional controversialists. The incident on '3-1252' gave them full scope: it could not have happened as I said; the inspector did not know what he was doing; it was not surprising something broke, because Blondel was driving the engine all wrong anyway! Fortunately there were others who took the other side, and I spent hours drafting my own replies; and in the meantime the editor, dear old Lough Pendred—one of the greatest friends I have ever had in the journalistic world—just sat back and enjoyed it all!

The twenty-ninth of June 1937 was a day to remember. The LMS had entered upon the new streamlined race to the north, and on that day the Press and many other guests were taken on a high-speed run from Euston to Crewe and back with the new Coronation Scot train. I was one of those favoured with an invitation, and Derek Barrie, then in the publicity department of the LMS, arranged that the first two compartments of the leading coach should be kept for those intending to compile detailed logs. He and I had the two window corners, facing the engine. With him were Simon Corbett, then in the operating department, and the doyen of all train-timers, the late Cecil J. Allen. With me was W. H. McCormick, the kindly editor of the *Meccano Magazine*, who published many of my early articles, and to whom I shall always be grateful for the improvement of my English! He was always insistent upon the most faultless syntax.

We made a fast, though not exceptional, run as far north as Stafford, but then, down the magnificently straight stretch of the Madeley Bank, where, according to one of the 'old wives' tales' of the early railways, Francis Trevithick's 8 ft 6 in. single *Cornwall* was said to have travelled at 117 m.p.h., an attempt was to be made on the authentic British railway speed record—then standing at 113 m.p.h. and held by the LNER streamlined engine *Silver Fox*. On the footplate of the new LMS engine *Coronation* was Robin Riddles, then Principal Assistant to the Chief Mechanical Engineer; the driver and fireman were Tom Clarke and C. Fleet of Crewe North shed, and the fourth man was Inspector Sam Miller, of Willesden. They had definite instructions to try and get 120 m.p.h.; and so, after we had swept over the summit at Whitmore, the tremendous acceleration began. I was a little surprised and disappointed that speed had not been worked up to the full 90 m.p.h. permitted at this point, though even 85 m.p.h. over Whitmore was startling enough by the standards of 1937.

It has never been difficult for me to relive the excitement of the next few minutes, knowing what those on the footplate had been told to try and attain; though my own excitement, and that of the others who were stop-watching, was held in suspense as, with faces glued to the windows, we sighted and clocked the ever-faster flash-by of the mileposts—95 m.p.h., 100, 105 and then, acceleration slackening, 110. Another reading, 112½, and we were only two miles from the centre of Crewe: no record, by my reckoning, and we had not even equalled *Silver Fox*. Then in a flash thoughts turned to other things. We were still travelling very fast. So far the brakes seemed to have made little impression. The next minute could have seen the end of many of us, because for operating convenience that special was routed into a platform that meant traversing three crossovers in succession—*three*!

We struck the first one at 57 m.p.h. and, thanks to the superb track and the riding qualities of the locomotive, we got through safely—indeed we, in the front coach, felt little discomfort. But although the brakes really had us by then, the second crossover and then the third set us rocking so violently from side to side that for a few seconds I thought we should turn over. What we experienced however was nothing to what happened towards the rear of the train. I was to learn some thirty years later that even if the locomotive holds the road when running too fast through a crossover it is no guarantee that the rest of the train will stay on the track, and the remark of a friend who was travelling in the middle of the Coronation Scot, that the floor of the dining car was 'strewn with a mosaic of broken crockery' tells its own tale. But by the grace of God we arrived, shaken but safe, in the centre of Crewe station. What an arrival! In a trice the hazards were pushed aside. We four stop-watchers compared notes, for Barrie would soon have the Press in his hair: we were unanimous on 112½ m.p.h. and that no record could be claimed. Farther down the platform I saw reporters rushing to telephone kiosks to be first with the news of what one newspaper at least called a 'mishap' on arrival, and in our own circle, near the engine, Cecil J. Allen studying his notes said 'Milepost 156 to Crewe in exactly 2 minutes—nobody will believe us when we tell them!' But there is no doubt it had been a terribly close call from disaster.

At a luncheon at the Crewe Arms Hotel, E. J. H. Lemon, a Vice-President of the LMS, strove skilfully and wittily to play down the risks that had so startlingly eventuated, and with good food and wine the company—most of them at any rate—were in a mellow frame of mind to make the journey back to Euston; though when Lemon added that we should go 'rather fast', Barrie remarked to me in a stage whisper 'I'm slipping at Kilburn'! But Lemon had a surprise for us in that after-luncheon speech. In the course of it he was handed a slip of paper. He read it, and a broad smile spread over his face. He said 'I've not been bribed', and went on to tell how the chart from the speed indicator on the locomotive had been examined, and the maximum was not 112½ but 114 m.p.h. To have said that the four of us who had been stop-watching were surprised would have been an understatement. If there had been such a pronounced peak as 114 it was remarkable that not one of the four of us had caught it. Working quite independently our results were absolutely uniform. But the LMS officially claimed 114 m.p.h. and neither Barrie and Corbett, as railway officers, nor Allen and I, as their guests, could well dispute it, though privately I think we all had our doubts.

What can happen when a train does 'come off', through taking a crossover road too fast, will always remain starkly vivid in my memory, since I was involved in such a derailment, at about 70 m.p.h., at Didcot in September 1967. I have told the technical story of this alarming affair in one of my later books, and how the train came to travel as it did. But the feeling I had in the moment of crisis can never be set down in cold print: how the coach in which I was riding was suddenly swept to the left; how amid loud crashes and

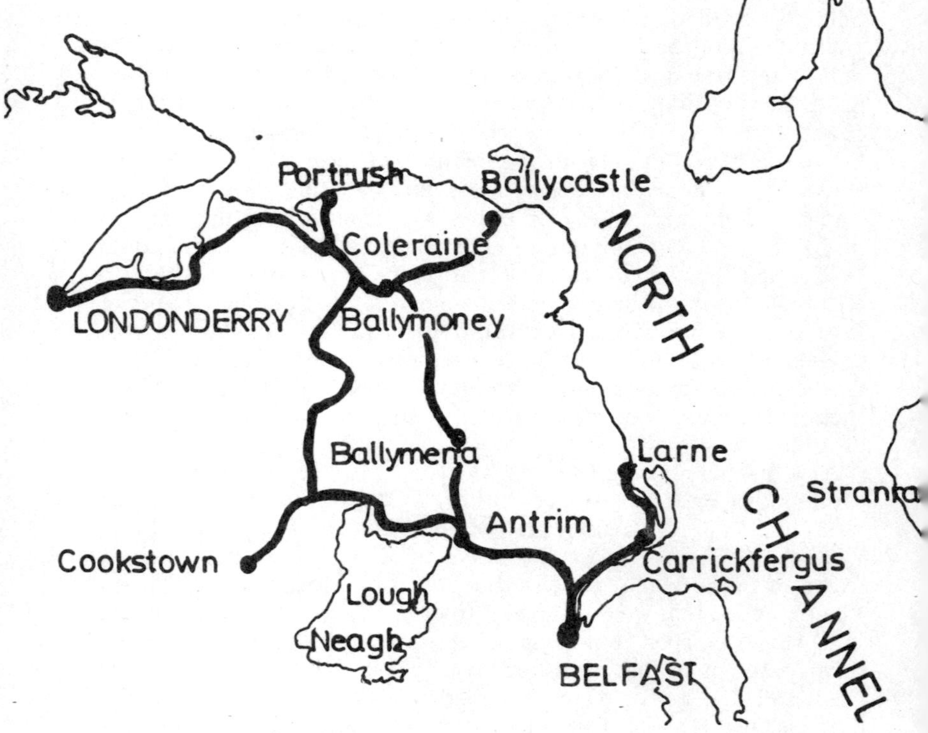


Fig. 1 The Northern Counties Committee (Northern Ireland) section of the LMSR

sickening lurches it was thrown from one side to the other, and how I got my feet wedged against the opposite seat to lessen the chance of my legs getting trapped, takes longer to write down than it did to happen. Then the coach came down on its right side. We were still travelling quite fast, and were dragged along in this way for a good quarter mile; but when we came to rest I realized I was safe and quite uninjured. The corridor side of the coach was upwards. I had been alone in the compartment and, making a ladder out of the seat cushions, and with the help of willing hands from above, I was able to get in the corridor and then jump down on to the track. The engine and the first five coaches had got safely through. The sixth had been partially derailed, but the last three had all come right off. The seventh and eighth—the last of which I was in—had had their bogies torn clean off, and the ninth, the last in the train, had broken away and turned over. What would have happened if the engine itself had turned over does not bear thinking about. The front coaches of the train were well crowded!

To revert now to the mid-1930s, it was about that time that W. A. Willox, editor of the *Railway Magazine*, asked me to do a comprehensive write-up on the Northern Counties Committee section of the LMSR. Northern Ireland was a happier place then than it is unfortunately today, and I had some very enjoyable visits. Major Malcolm Speir was then Manager and Secretary. He began on the Caledonian, and before going to Belfast he had already had a brilliant career as an operating officer, on the Highland, in Glasgow, and not least in the Railway Operating Division of the British Army during the First World War. Full of boundless energy, a veritable 'human dynamo', he was equally a great Christian gentleman, admired by all who worked under him. He was intensely proud of the NCC and had every facet of its working and engineering at his finger tips. On my first visit to Belfast, although I was only the veriest beginner in the literary world, he not only received me personally but summoned all the senior officers to a briefing session, and from that moment I had the freedom of the railway. Seen in retrospect it was an exacting assignment. My professional duties kept my nose very close to the grindstone in London, just round the corner from the offices of my present kind publisher. The only time I had available was one free Saturday a month, with the occasional bank holiday weekend.

How I enjoyed those visits to Ireland! I used to travel by the Ulster Express from Euston on Friday evenings, sleep and breakfast on the Heysham boat, and be in the Belfast offices as soon as the staff arrived. I travelled all over the line: to Londonderry, Portrush, Cookstown, Larne, over the deeply rural Derry Central line on the footplate of an old two-cylinder compound 2–4–0, down the narrow-gauge Ballycastle line. 'The Major', as Speir was known up and down the line, was an immaculate operator. Every train ran on the stroke of time. Five minutes was enough margin for connecting services at junctions, and at Larne harbour he installed a belt conveyor for luggage and mails so that the Stranraer steamer could sail *eight minutes* after the boat train from Belfast arrived. Yes, eight minutes! I watched it happen, and participated several times and could not help thinking of the endless delays and confusion at the Channel Ports. True, there was no customs examination at Larne Harbour, but the steamers were just as large and carried just as many people as those that crossed the English Channel.

Many years later there was an amusing sequel to that journalistic commission of the 'thirties, which can be told now. It was just after the end of the Second World War and I had been to Belfast to give one of the Christmas Lectures of the Institution of Civil Engineers. A senior railwayman I had met during that earlier commission was in the audience and, learning I was bound for Glasgow that evening, asked me to join him on the journey. Once again I was given the freedom of the NCC, but in more convivial circumstances. At Larne we joined in the snappy dash from train to boat, but this time I was taken straight up to the Captain, and hospitality began to flow freely. It was a wild January night. I have the reputation of being a good sailor, but this was going to be a supreme test! After two very large whiskys, someone with a sense of humour and a determination to see whether their visitor's head was as strong and unshakable as his sea-legs said 'I expect Mr Nock would like to see the engine room.' Really I could not have cared less, but down we went, and as by that time the ship was out into the full force of the gale our progress was a bit uncertain, not helped by the many passengers already prostrate in varying degrees of seagoing misery on stairways and in passages.

Below, amid the whirr of the turbines and the enthusiasm of those who showed me round, my feelings weie light-headed, rather than those of *mal de mer*, although the ship was performing all sorts of antics. It was worse when we went up aloft again, this time to the bridge, but not before there had been more hospitality on the way! What a night! The crossing from Larne to Stranraer takes only two hours, but packet steamers have been lost in those wild waters, and up on the bridge we had the full benefit of the rolling and pitching. But my stomach did not let me down, and the last half hour in sheltered water passed pleasantly. I was still feeling somewhat gay, under the influence of their whisky, when I stepped ashore; but my next assignment, and at once, was on the footplate, and after no more than twenty minutes of a 'Black Five' 4–6–0 I was as sober as any judge. I must not digress into Scottish locomotive experiences at this stage however.

Back to the NCC. One Saturday morning, having travelled overnight from London, I was to ride the engine of the Portrush Flyer, one of Malcolm Speir's prestige express trains. Whatever may have happened elsewhere in Ireland, there was no dawdling by the wayside on his railway, and this was particularly interesting to me, because quite half the run to Portrush was made over single line. The locomotives were fitted with the Manson apparatus for mechanical exchange of the tokens at full speed; and on the Portrush run single line working began at Ballymena. I was riding on the tender, where I could look ahead over the driver's shoulder, and the approach to Ballymena station is over a considerable right-hand curve, intersected by several points and crossings. Suddenly a heftier bang than usual made the tender give a jump, and it sent the hinged fallplate of the engine flying up and over, and it hit and jammed the mechanical token exchanger, down on the left hand side of the cab beside the driver. He seized a hammer and attacked it viciously, but it could not be freed in time, and we ran past the lineside standard without collecting the token. We had to stop for the fireman to go back and get it.

Catching trains, not to mention tokens, had its moments in Ireland. One bank holiday weekend I was staying at a small hotel just beside the station in Portrush, and I took a day off to see something of the beautiful coastal scenery. On the previous evening I was at pains to tell the porter that I did not want calling till eight o'clock, but instead there was a tremendous tattoo on my door at six-thirty. We both enjoyed the joke, but that evening before going to bed I said to him 'Now look here, Paddy, I don't want any mistakes tomorrow. I really *do* want calling at six-thirty, because I am catching the train to Belfast.' I was actually going right through to London in the day, because by one of Malcolm Speir's snappy connections, the 8.10 a.m. North Atlantic Express arrived in Belfast ten minutes before the Larne boat train left. Actually the same set of coaches was used for both trains. On the connecting train the other side there was a through carriage from Stranraer to Euston, attached to the Midday Scot, at Carlisle. Next morning there was no call at all. It was high summer and I was fortunately awake in plenty of time. I dressed, breakfasted, and went across to the station. Just before the guard's whistle blew the hotel porter came dashing and breathless down the platform, gasping 'Och, it's moighty glad I am you've caught your train, bedad'!

Farther south in Ireland the old Great Southern and Western Railway prided itself on its mechanical engineering prowess. At Inchicore Works, Dublin, shop practice was based upon that of Crewe; but from 1913, after R. E. L. Maunsell had left to become Chief Mechanical Engineer of the South Eastern and Chatham Railway, to quote a poetic member of the staff 'There arose a new king over Egypt who knew not Joseph', and for some years things went sadly awry. Large new engines were built, and were soon in dead trouble. Scapegoats were sought, though the fault lay at the top; old and trusted men were fired. It was an unhappy time, and the inheritors in the 1920s were concerned mostly with salvage. By the time I first went to Cork, however, in the mid-1930s, the old efficiency had largely returned, though at times the locomotives were underpowered for the work they had to do. The English Mail was as much a prestige job as the Irish Mail was on this side of the water, and one afternoon, on the platform of the Glanmire station, Cork, I witnessed a scene that belonged to another generation.

Stowing my effects, for I was not going to ride on the footplate all the way to Dublin, I was attracted by a furious row in progress—a one-sided row nevertheless. A first class passenger of the *ancien régime*—the Anglo-Irish as they were sometimes called then—was berating a very inoffensive middle-aged porter: 'You damned idiot,' he yelled, 'do as you're told!' Apparently the hapless man had loaded his extensive luggage into an ordinary first class compartment, whereas this 'superior person' wanted it in the dining car. The porter may have been a bit of a dumb-bunny, but I was amazed he took such a tirade in complete silence, and obediently shifted all the luggage. I hastened forward to the engines—yes, engines in the plural: we had *three* that afternoon!

Starting out of Cork towards Dublin is like going up the side of a house. From the very platform end the line disappears into a long tunnel, and through that tunnel the gradient is 1 in 60. The train, weighing a little under 400 tons, was not heavy for that era but, on the Great Southern, with the limited engine power they had then, it was a problem. A 4–6–0, salvaged and much improved from the errors of the post-Maunsell period, was to take the train through to Dublin, but on the long rises leading to the central tableland of south-east Ireland it was not enough and a 4–4–0 was coupled ahead to help as far as Ballybrophy. But even these two would not manage that first fearful climb through the tunnel, and in front of them was the third engine, an old six-coupled goods that would help as far as Blarney. What a sight the three of them must have looked as we came out of that tunnel, puffing and panting, doing little more than 20 m.p.h. and steam spurting from the two old engines in front in all sorts of places whence it should not have come!

That journey could nevertheless have been almost ordained by providence to provide a blinding contrast to an experience I was to have two years later. Then, at last, Inchicore had come into its own again. The new Chief Mechanical Engineer, Edgar C. Bredin, had produced a splendid new 4–6–0 locomotive, equal in power to most of the largest British engines of the day. There were no mistakes this time: the mourning, as it were, of the prevailing all-black livery was cast aside, and '800' was decked in a lovely blue-green, and named *Maeve*, after one of the queens of ancient Irish history. Bredin cordially agreed to my request for some footplate passes, but it was not until the middle of August 1939 that I was able to go. Then the times were very troubled. It was not only the awful threat and virtual certainty of European war. The IRA were active, and not many days before I went to Dublin I had been near enough to a bomb explosion in the cloakroom at King's Cross station, in which a man was killed and many others injured, for my face to be blackened with the dust thrown up.

As usual then my rides on *Maeve* had to be fixed for a Saturday, and traffic for the morning mail from Dublin was so heavy that the train was run in two parts. *Maeve* had the first, with no more than a moderate tonnage, and we had a very easy and comfortable run. It did not tell me very much, except that she was an elegant riding and very fast engine; but coming back in the late afternoon it was different—very, *very* different. An eastbound transatlantic liner had put in at Cobh, formerly Queenstown, setting ashore many passengers by tender; extra coaches were to be added to the English Mail to take them to Dublin and, with this and many holiday makers hurrying home before the gathering storm, the train was to be loaded to 450 tons. Down at the shed it was agreed that *Maeve* should take this *unassisted*, whereas two years ago a load of 390 tons had needed three engines! All the elements of an exciting occasion were present. While Inspector Murphy had come down from Dublin with me in the morning, we were joined by three others in the cab to see how the engine took that villainous first gradient: the District Locomotive Superintendent, his chief inspector, and the Glanmire Shed foreman, making with the driver and fireman seven of us in the cab. The sense of occasion was completed by the crowd of sightseers on the platform, which I was told gathered every afternoon to see *Maeve*.

The driver and fireman, Foley and Ryan, of Inchicore, were experts of the highest order, and with such a load and in such conditions there was only one way to handle an engine—flat out! Into the tunnel we went. The percussion was terrific. In the glare from the firedoor anxious faces watched the needle of the pressure gauge; but I was wondering what would happen if that great engine lost her feet and began slipping. We should surely have stalled. But all was well, and we came into the open at Kilbarry doing nearly 24 m.p.h., with the exhaust from the chimney shooting straight up. Mark Foley eased the throttle back a bit once that first fearful incline was surmounted, but then—one of those snags on a new engine—he could not get it open again until he had shut off steam altogether, still on a rising gradient. We lost a little time to our first stop, Mallow; but then, having said farewell to our three local visitors, Foley and Ryan made a magnificent run to Dublin.

I shall not forget the arrival there, nor the run down to Dun Laoghaire to catch the mail boat for Holyhead. Most of the coaches in our train, including the mail vans, were going down to the pier station. They were already packed, but a tremendous crowd was waiting at Kingsbridge station, and the train was simply besieged. When I had taken leave of my friends on the engine the train was jammed from end to end, and nobody wanted to—or indeed could—make room for a very dirty fellow in overalls, still less make way, once he was on board, for him to get to a lavatory and wash. At Dun Laoghaire I went on to the boat as I had climbed down from *Maeve*. Fortunately I knew some of the ship's officers, or it might have been difficult to convince them I was not on the run having just blown up a bank, or something.

# 3 The Broadening Prospect

That day with *Maeve* was for me the end of a chapter. The night Irish Mail landed me back in Euston before breakfast, and the Sunday papers were full of alarms and excursions—with good reason. Within three weeks Hitler had loosed the Luftwaffe upon Poland, and within days we too were at war. For a time 'out the line' became a thing of the past for me; but, by the strangest twist of circumstance, the outbreak of war and the move of the Westinghouse London office staff from King's Cross to Chippenham, in Wiltshire, coincided with my being given the most important literary commission I had yet received, and one that was to have far-reaching consequences. At that time *The Engineer* was not only the oldest but probably also the most influential technical journal of any in the world; but what was more remarkable was that the editorship had been in one family for seventy years, and was to continue so for yet another twenty.

The Pendreds, father, son, and grandson, were no ordinary editors. They were professional engineers of very high status. At the time of my first contact with the great journal the son, Loughnan St Lawrence, was in the chair, sufficiently eminent to have been President of the Institution of Mechanical Engineers, and fortunate enough to have held that high honour in the year that the Institution was granted its Royal Charter. Lough Pendred himself was one of the most delightful characters who ever graced the literary world of engineering. He had all the wit of his Irish ancestry, and its sense of fun, combined with superb professionalism on technical matters, and an immense breadth of outlook. To be interviewed by him and charged with a commission to write something was exhilarating. With him there was never the fear that half one's script would receive the order of the blue pencil; one felt he was inviting you to co-operate.

During the war at his invitation I wrote several series of articles, all on signalling and allied subjects, and for various reasons they appeared anonymously; but in 1944 came his suggestion that really sent me 'out the line'. Locomotive operation in Great Britain at that time in the war was probably more difficult than at any time previously in the history of our railways. Pendred thought it would be good to lay some of the inside story bare, as indicating both strengths and weaknesses in design practices, workshop techniques and so on. I protested mildly that I should only be able to go out at weekends, but he gaily waved this aside saying 'Couldn't be better. You'll see things at their worst.' The railways were ready enough to co-operate, and so I set out, under the extraordinary travelling conditions of war and the immediate post-war period, to make journeys on locomotives that took me from my wartime home in Chippenham, Wiltshire, to Plymouth, to West Wales, to Glasgow several times, to Aberdeen, to East Anglia, and in many other places where the going was tough. The result was a series of technical articles that went on for more than two years, because when the war was over, things for a time got worse, not better!

I could write whole chapters about the adventures I had travelling, as passenger, to my selected test routes; of the problems of getting accommodation for the night, and *food.* Just imagine a time when having, well in advance, reserved a room in a first class hotel, one had also, equally well in advance, to reserve a place for dinner! Sometimes, at some brief staging point, one would arrive in a town to find not a single café open. I would arrive late at night in the blackout, to pick my way through unfamiliar streets. The crowding in trains was at times just unbelievable. I remember having to board a train in the early hours of the morning. I opened a door leading into the corridor, and a sailor, dead asleep, rolled out on to the platform. A friend, boarding an eastbound night train at Plymouth, found the only place she could sit was in the gangway connection between two carriages! Very often I prolonged my stay on the footplate because it was the only place where there was any room. The technical data I collected was amazing in its variety. There were engines that despite their shabby exterior were in first-rate mechanical condition; others were incredibly off-beat. The quality of coal was often deplorable, while a recurring difficulty was that of engines overdue for boiler wash-out, and with blocked tubes, making the steaming unreliable. But these are technicalities. The human side was invariably fascinating.

One of my earliest journeys was on a Great Western 'Castle' class engine working through from Shrewsbury to Newton Abbot. In pre-war years the running of the through expresses on the service from Liverpool and Manchester to Devon and Cornwall had been a prestige job, shared, as far as the Great Western was concerned, between Shrewsbury and Newton Abbot sheds; and for some reason, when most other lodging turns had been suspended, this one had remained. Despite war conditions both sheds seem to vie with one another as to which could turn out the smartest engine. However grimed and shabby other engines might be, the one for this duty, at each shed, had to be immaculate. The old sense of pride in the job was never far below the surface with British railwaymen. It certainly crystallized out in the preparation of these engines. After all that we had endured in the war years the sight of that engine, the *Usk Castle*, at Newton Abbot was the tonic of the year for me, and the performance on the long run up to Shrewsbury was faultless. It was typical of the period that we had many delays on the way, because passenger trains did not have their one-time priority in the autumn of 1944. But when we did get a clear road, as in the heavy hill-climbing through the Welsh border country, through Abergavenny, past the Sugar Loaf Mountain, and up the long rise from Ludlow into the Stretton Hills, the going was superb.

It was a condition of the facilities I was given that my scripts were submitted to authority before publication, and I was not unduly surprised that the one describing the southbound run from Shrewsbury took a little time to come back to me, eventually with no comment except formal approval. Many years later I learned that my account had caused some consternation at Swindon. They could not believe engines were still doing so well, so late in the war. The testing staff were not busy at the time, and a little team was sent out to check up on the same train and engine. They returned to report that the going was even better than on my trip.

On a lowering November day in 1945 I was at Crewe ready to ride the engine of the wartime Royal Scot through to Glasgow. The engine worked over the entire 401 miles, but was then re-manned at Crewe, and I met the fresh pair of enginemen on the platform before the train arrived from London. Typical Glaswegians, the driver was a dry, taciturn though friendly enough little Scot; the fireman, talkative and very intelligent, gave me his views on various locomotive designs, and I was rather shocked when he referred to the 'Baby Scots'—distinctly one of my own favourite classes—as the 'wur-r-rld's wust'. I must admit, however, that by then some of them probably were! Further reminiscences were cut short by the arrival of the train from London. The engine, the *City of Nottingham*, was one of the 'Duchess' class, similar to the *Coronation* of 1937, but non-streamlined. Externally I should not think it had seen a cleaner's rag for weeks, and with it having been running the 401 miles between London and Glasgow nearly every day, in rough autumnal weather, the normal stains of fast travel on top of the dirt gave a most woebegone appearance to such a fine engine. The moment she stopped there was a minor emergency. One of the water gauge glasses was broken, and a new one had to be fitted while the train was waiting at the platform. It was done with swift efficiency, and off we set, non-stop to Carlisle.

It was an afternoon of miserable weather, no occasion for record-breaking even if the timetable had required it. But the engine was a thoroughbred, beneath her coating of grime, and save in one very disconcerting respect she gave an immaculate performance. It was the first time I had been on this class of engine, and we had not travelled far before I noticed how the exhaust steam from the very short chimney was clinging to the top of the boiler and flopping down over the cab—at times completely obscuring the look-out ahead. Like all the best of his kind our driver knew the route almost blindfold, but there were many times when he had to shut off steam in order to get a sight of the signals. Of course the cold, damp atmosphere made things much worse, and there were times when such necessary adjustment meant loss of speed on a rising gradient. I put in a private report to H. G. Ivatt, then Chief Mechanical Engineer of the LMS, and was very glad when some months later they began fitting smoke deflecting shields on either side of the smokeboxes of these engines. It made a tremendous difference. On this first trip of mine conditions got worse as we went north into Scotland; but what a change came over that once-taciturn little driver. Back in his native land he sang to us, and we climbed the Beattock Bank to recitations from Burns!

In Glasgow there was just time for a late 'tea' with some Scottish friends: 'tea', that amazing meal taken at any time between 5 p.m. and midnight, and with a menu, even in 1945, enough to fortify one for several days. On this occasion I could not linger, for I was returning south on the engine of the 'Ghost Train'. Let me explain: during the war when everyone was asked 'Is your journey really necessary?', or to 'Give your seat to a shell', some 'speerin' body'—to use the Scots vernacular—discovered there was a train leaving Euston for the north that was not in the timetable, and carrying his speerin' a bit further found that it ran every night! Someone was bending the rules, and 'Paul Pry' told his M.P. about it. Sure enough there came a question in the House of Commons, when it transpired that this heavy sleeping express was run between London and Glasgow purely for services personnel. After this public revelation of its existence, it became known as the Ghost Train. In Scotland it ran over the former Glasgow and South Western line, to serve Dumfries and Kilmarnock, both of which had heavy military traffic at that time, and it terminated at St Enoch station, in Glasgow.

I had always felt at home at St Enoch from a time going back about fifteen years earlier, when I had spent some time measuring up 'out the line' ready for the installation of colour-light signals and electric points. I became so involved at one time that a wag in the London office of Westinghouse suggested that the name of the station should be changed to 'St O. Nock'. But when I came to ride the engine of the Ghost Train I had some difficulty in persuading the ticket collector to let me through the barrier. An engine pass cut no ice with him. I was a civilian, and not a railway servant either. However, all was well in the end, and I climbed aboard one of the streamlined LMS 'Pacifics'. The driver and fireman this time were broad Cumbrians. In pre-grouping days the Carlisle running sheds of the Glasgow and South Western Railway were at Currock Road, south of the city, and unlike the Caledonian men up at Kingmoor, two miles to the north, who were essentially Borderers, most of the 'Sou' West' men at Currock Road were strong north-country English.

Our driver that night, Johnny Cartmell, was a great chap and a supreme engineman. As on the northbound run earlier that day the engine, the *Princess Alexandra*, was going right through to London; but Cartmell and his fireman were being relieved at Carlisle. From the passenger point of view the train was non-stop from Dumfries to Watford, and the stop at Carlisle, in the early hours of the morning, was made not in the station but at the former London and North Western engine sheds, at Upperby Bridge, about a mile to the south. I was finishing my footplate work at Carlisle, and Cartmell suggested that to save me the mile walk back to the station in the darkness I might be prepared to nip off, as they ran through the platform. 'We're nearly always checked by signal and sometimes stopped' he added. And so, with the *Princess Alexandra* slowed down to 10 m.p.h., at about 1 a.m., I took my leave of the 'Ghost Train' as it ran through Carlisle station.

But bed was still 141 miles away, in the Crewe Arms Hotel. In less than half an hour in came the night Birmingham Scotsman, first stop Crewe, but one look at the coaches decided me that the most comfortable place to ride would be on the engine, this time one of the incomparable 'Black Five' 4–6–0s. I say 'incomparable', and so they were, as ever-willing, longsuffering workhorses, capable of taking any amount of hard flogging, running immense mileages between repairs, and requiring a minimum amount of routine attention. For this very reason they were rarely limousines to ride: they rattled and banged their way along, and it was usually far pleasanter to stand than to sit on the tip-up seats provided. Their vibration could go through every nerve in your body. The driver and fireman were a cheery pair, and laughed their heads off when I showed my pass and said I thought I should be more comfortable with them than cramped up in the corridor of a very crowded train. I was nearly asleep on my feet before we got to Crewe, and apart from the technical details of the run, which I conscientiously entered into my notebook, the most lasting recollection of the trip is of the driver's love of the whistle. At every junction, and particularly at big stations like Carnforth, Lancaster and Wigan, he punctuated the stillness of the night with a long-sustained blast on our deep bass hooter.

Many of my most lasting memories of those years are of journeys in Scotland, but I must interpose the recollection of an incident in Ireland, not long after the war. By the strangest of coincidences I was invited to give two lectures, one to the Royal Dublin Society, and one one of the Christmas holiday lectures for boys organized by the Institution of Civil Engineers, on that occasion in Belfast. How they came to fall upon two successive days I cannot now remember; but fall they did, and I combined with them business in Doncaster and Glasgow. The London and North Eastern Railway had just put into commission a somewhat revolutionary form of panel interlocking at Doncaster, and representing *The Engineer* I went with a party of technical journalists. Wearing my other hat, as a Westinghouse man, it was not a system of signalling that we liked very much, and it proved to be the only one of its kind ever installed. It was not an easy thing to describe, even to one familiar with signalling practice. Heading west for Ireland afterwards I travelled as far as Manchester with the Special Correspondent of *The Times*, and he put me through a searching cross-examination. He was obviously floundering, and when we parted he said 'Don't laugh too much when you read my article.'

I crossed by the mail steamer from Holyhead to Dun Laoghaire that night and, once arrived in Dublin, the year being 1948, my hosts took it for granted that anyone from England was starving, and laid on the most colossal meals. Had I done anything like full justice to them I should have been so stupefied as to be incapable of lecturing at all. In the audience at the Royal Dublin Society was Edgar Bredin, designer of *Maeve*, and his wife; and during a little party afterwards she told me a good story. After leaving the Kingsbridge terminus the main line to Cork climbs a steep gradient, and with heavy trains it had become usual during the war to provide a pusher engine in rear. The Bredins lived in a house overlooking the line, and they had a young maid who was something of a railway enthusiast and a staunch supporter of *Maeve* and her two royal sisters. One morning while they were at breakfast this girl dashed in almost speechless with excitement. When she had recovered her breath sufficiently to speak she told, with eyes shining, how *Maeve* had just taken the mail up the hill so fast that the pusher engine had got left about a coach length's behind, and could not catch up!

On the following day I had an experience that taught me a lesson.

My friends at the Royal Dublin Society had been careful to impress upon me the need to get my lantern slides carefully booked in at Dun Laoghaire, otherwise I should have difficulty in getting them out of Eire afterwards, thanks to customs regulations. I was travelling to Belfast and had no difficulties on leaving Eire, at Dundalk. But it had not occurred to me that I ought also to have had them duly checked *out* of the United Kingdom at Holyhead, and when it came to entering Northern Ireland, at Goraghwood, I was in dead trouble. My luggage containing the slides was immediately impounded, and the only concession made at the border station was that it was put into the custody of the guard, to be handed over to the Customs on arrival in Belfast. So here was I arriving to give a lecture on behalf of the Institution of Civil Engineers that same afternoon, with my entire luggage in quarantine, as it were. Fortunately my host was the Chief Engineer of the Port of Belfast Authority, and the telephone lines to the Custom House almost took fire! The most resolute and determined of his assistants was despatched and told not to leave the Custom House until he had my suitcase. He stormed into the hall with the precious luggage, ten minutes *after* the meeting had started, and I was already on my feet, talking, minus the pictures!

This has necessarily been a chapter of mixed memories, and there is one more, of those days before the railways of Britain were nationalized—a real Sunday afternoon field day. The Great Western justifiably prided themselves on their record of safe operation, helped in no small measure by their system of automatic train control. In 1947 there were plans for introducing colour-light signalling with four aspects, including the preliminary warning of the 'double yellow' installed on the Southern at the time I was 'out the line' at Cannon Street. The Great Western felt it desirable to distinguish between the two degrees of warning presented by the lineside 'double yellow' and 'single yellow' aspects in the audible signals given in the engine cab, and by some careful experimenting and design it was found possible to give a double 'toot-toot' on the warning siren to correspond with a double yellow signal. Development had reached the stage where the technical press were invited to a demonstration, and I went representing *The Engineer*.

At that time speed everywhere on the Great Western was limited to a maximum of 75 m.p.h., but as a pointer to future development a stretch of the up main line between Reading and Maidenhead was specially fettled up to permit, on this one special occasion, much higher speeds. It was hoped to demonstrate the 'double toot' cab indication at 90 m.p.h., or perhaps even more. A special train was run consisting of the dynamometer car for the testing staff, two of the luxurious saloons used on the Ocean Mail specials for the invited guests, and a brake-third in rear. To haul it was a 'Castle' class engine, the *Earl of Powys*, polished as though she was to work the Royal Train. The test began at Reading, but from the viewpoint of speed records it was unfortunate that the Civil Engineer could not relax the speed limit through Twyford station, 5 miles on our way, which had to remain at 75 m.p.h.; but after that we could run.

So that the audible signals received in the engine cab could be heard by all of us travelling in the train a system of loudspeakers had been fitted up, and as we got away from Reading we heard clearly the short loud ring of the bell each time we passed a clear signal, and an observer on the engine announced the speed. We passed through Twyford, and then we really began to go. That day I had with me a split-second chronograph and succeeding miles were covered at 83.4 m.p.h., 87.3, 90.5, 93.3, and finally 95.2 m.p.h. Then came a fine demonstration of the 'double toot', the brakes were applied, and we stopped smoothly in Maidenhead station. The maximum speed measured in the dynamometer car was 96½ m.p.h. Many years later I learned of a very amusing sidelight on this test. A great friend, then in the Signal Department of the Great Western, was detailed off to make some lineside observations on the track east of Twyford. He took his wife with him, and instructed her how to take a photograph of the train as it passed. She was so staggered at the speed it came up that she did not 'snap' much more than the tail lamp!

# 4 A Scottish Miscellany

Early in my railway explorations in Great Britain I went to see the most magnificently scenic route in all Britain, the West Highland, and its extension to Mallaig. Whole books have been written about the history, construction and operating features of the nigh 100 mile section between Helensburgh and Fort William. One can be so rapt in its scenic glories as to be oblivious of anything else; and the passing scene is never the same on two successive journeys, under those capricious Highland skies. But of all my visits that during the Easter weekend of 1946 remains most vividly in mind. I had stayed overnight in Glasgow, and rose early to catch the 5 a.m. train to Fort William, riding on the footplate from the very start. We had one of the Gresley three-cylinder 'K 4' 2–6–0s, the *Cameron of Lochiel*, and when at daybreak we had run down beside the River Clyde, with its manifold industrial activities, we passed through the junction at Craigendoran and headed at once into the pure mountain glory of the West Highlands, white with hoar frost under a cloudless dawn sky.

We had not gone far when memory received a jolt. Up in the heather, above Garelochhead, a labouring squad of German prisoners of war was at work on the line. It was the first time I had been up the West Highland since the bad days of September 1938, and then, with a Sunday to spare during a business visit to Scotland, I had taken the day excursion from Glasgow to Fort William and Mallaig. But there was no enjoyment to be had from the trip that day. The mountains, moors, and sea lochs passed no more than vaguely before me. Thoughts were constantly on how soon we might be at war, and what that would bring to my family and me. A few days later Chamberlain flew to Berchtesgaden. This stark memory came back in a flash when I saw those chaps at work by the lineside, and recalled momentarily all that had happened in the years between. But in 1946 on the footplate of the *Cameron of Lochiel* there were immediate problems to rivet my attention. She was not steaming well, and the long grind up Glen Falloch, from the head of Loch Lomond, is no place for an ailing engine. The fireman was working like a

Trojan, but what the Scots call a 'dreich steamer' needs brains as well as brawn, and this man just had not got it. Up those wicked 1 in 60 gradients, round the incessant curves, over high lattice girder bridges we laboured on and only just managed to scramble over the top and into the welcome ten-minute stop at Crianlarich. A young apprentice from Doncaster took my place on the footplate after this, while I enjoyed a snack breakfast in the train, and revelled in the glorious scenery.

Hoping to get some more satisfactory data for the technical article I had in mind, I arranged to ride back as far as Crianlarich on the southbound afternoon train, and there to intercept the last train down from Glasgow to return to Fort William for the night. I was at first dismayed to see that the engine was once again the *Cameron of Lochiel*, but this time with Fort William men, instead of the Glasgow crew that had worked north that morning. We were not five miles on our way before I was scarcely believing it was the same engine. It was an absolute joy to ride with two men who put such guts, zest, and downright intelligence into their work. 'Dreich steamer' my foot—not with such a fireman as Rogers on the shovel, and it was not with any kid-gloves treatment that he was working. Geordie Clarkson the driver had time to make up, and he *flailed* the engine up those West Highland hills; and while giving him plenty of steam Rogers had time to tell me of his first time out as a driver. I should explain he had reached the grade of 'passed fireman', and could if need be take charge of an engine in traffic. One very bad winter's day he was ordered out with a snow plough. There was a bad block up in the mountains, and he was sent to try and clear it. The only 'fireman' that could be found for him was a very young cleaner, who had never previously been outside the shed yard. The going was pretty rough, and once up into the blizzard snow was driving into the cab and clogging up everywhere; soon the hapless youth was shovelling more snow than coal into the firebox! Ordinarily Rogers was the kind of man who could drive *and fire* an engine singlehanded; but he had a job on that day. I have found it typical that the finest enginemen can quickly inspire confidence in the greenest novice. So it was with Rogers, and it was Geordie Clarkson who told me that before they won back to Fort William his mate was firing like a veteran.

On this single-tracked railway we were booked to cross the down train at Ardlui, where Clarkson and Rogers would exchange engines with the Glasgow men. By way of a break, because I had been footplating with no more than short intervals since five o'clock that morning, Inspector Graham and I left the *Cameron of Lochiel* at Crianlarich and had a cup of tea and a snack in the refreshment room, while our friends coasted down Glen Falloch, took over the down train engine, and then shovelled their way back up that tough gradient. They arrived just under an hour later with an engine of the same class, the *Lord of the Isles*, and the atmosphere was tense. The blower was on, and boiler pressure was well down. Taking over an ailing engine in mid-stream, as it were, is no joke and Rogers had had no time to get the fire into decent shape; but the ten-minute refreshment stop for the passengers gave him a chance, and he worked assiduously. Steam pressure was still well below normal when we got the right away; but, as if to say 'forget that thing', he hung his coat over the pressure gauge as Geordie thrashed the engine up the hill towards Tyndrum. Up the exposed mountainside we pounded; over those slender lattice-girdered viaducts, with the burns below swollen into so many rampaging torrents, the wind and the rain caught us viciously. Meanwhile Rogers had worked to some purpose, and nearing Tyndrum to the delight of us all that apparently ailing engine blew off. Despite the hard work up the gradient he had rallied the boiler to full pressure.

We crossed the Perth–Argyll county march at 1,024 feet above sea level and coasted down to the Horseshoe Bend. The dark majesty of the glen was awe-inspiring. Thick rain-laden clouds were drifting up the flanks of Ben Doran, and the gloom in the corries was intense. Just north of the Horseshoe red deer were feeding on the moorland; two of them, one a big fellow with fine antlers, were actually on the track, and leapt nimbly over the fence as we bore down upon them. So, in typical West Highland weather, by mountain, moor, and loch, we made our way back to Fort William, to arrive, as usual when Clarkson and Rogers were on the job, on time.

In popular parlance the word 'wash-out' is used to describe a disastrous occasion or some inept organization or individual; but to a railwayman the term is literal, and means the destruction of a part of the line by some natural cause, usually by flooding. It is the kind of incident that is much more frequent in countries subject to extremes of climate and rainfall, and such railways are engineered to provide against the damage of exceptional flooding, as at the time of the monsoon in India, or during seasonal rains in Africa and Australia. But even so there are times when the flood waters get beyond control; embankments are washed away with the rails left hanging, bridges are destroyed, and wholesale disruption of service is caused. Such incidents are happily rare in Great Britain, though in 1914, following a cloudburst in East Inverness-shire, a bridge on the Highland main line was washed away and part of a train fell into the breach. But I was involved in the aftermath of a far more dramatic washout, or series of washouts, in 1948. In the autumn of that year I rode the engine of the Flying Scotsman southbound from Edinburgh, by a most unusual route. It took us over the Lammermuir Hills to Galashiels, past Melrose and St Boswells, on through Kelso, and finally down the Tweed Valley to rejoin the East Coast main line at Tweedmouth Junction, just south of Berwick. It was a procedure needed for nearly three months after the most extraordinary incident in the entire history of railways in Great Britain. I use the word 'incident' as it became familiar in civil defence parlance during the Second World War, when an incident was anything from a fire that could be put out with nothing more than a couple of stirrup-pumps to the devastation caused by a V2 rocket. It was the time of the summer service, and the Flying Scotsman had for the first time since the war resumed non-stop running between London and Edinburgh. The afternoon of 12 August, most unkindly for the opening of the grouse-shooting season, was stormy up in the north-east; but the 'non-stop' was on time, and going well. She was north of Alnmouth however when news of a washout south of Berwick led to her being stopped and instructed to return to Newcastle. News of what proved to be no more than a minor breach in the line reached Control in time for three succeeding expresses to be sent across to Carlisle to take the former North British line, the 'Waverley Route', northwards to Edinburgh. When the Flying Scotsman had eventually been drawn back to Newcastle, it was to find she was then the fourth in the procession of Anglo-Scottish expresses from King's Cross taking this roundabout route.

That small washout in Northumberland, which was the original cause of these diversions, was providential, for few of the passengers or the train crews could in their wildest imagination have pictured what had happened north of Berwick. The storms of that afternoon culminated in a veritable cloudburst—'to end all other cloudbursts', as one of my railway friends afterwards expressed it. It burst over the Lammermuir Hills, and water poured over the open hillsides in such volume and with such violence as to suggest that a dam had been breached. But it was just rain—rain that registered a fall of 6 in. at Kelso within twenty-four hours. Grim stories of the breaching of dams by aerial attack during the war were still fresh in mind, and the cataracts that poured over the hills overlooking the railway at Grantshouse were simply terrifying. Near the station is the summit point of the line between Berwick and Edinburgh, and the flood waters divided and went north and south. In the five miles between Grantshouse and Reston the railway crosses the Eye Water seven times, and every one of these bridges was swept away, and the rails left hanging in mid-air. Massive stone structures were tumbled, like a child's building blocks, and at the southern end of this trail of disaster a danger even more terrible began to build up.

Between Reston Junction and the next station, Ayton, the railway is carried on a high embankment. Because of the collapse of a culvert there was no outlet for water rapidly collecting on the west side, and in a trough of the hills a great lake was formed, with the railway embankment acting as a dam. The water level rose steadily, and the great volume impounded was exerting tremendous pressure on a bank built more than a hundred years previously, purely to carry trains, not to have the resisting power of a great dam. If it had burst, nothing could have saved the little fishing port of Eyemouth from a fate like the German towns in the track of the released waters of Möhne. After surveys in the following days a trench fitted with sluice gates was cut through the embankment; 9 in. pipes were laid in, and much water was pumped away to safety. Gradually the danger was averted, but it had been a mighty close thing.

North of Grantshouse another torrent swept towards the sea, at Cockburnspath. Its first obstacle was Penmanshiel Tunnel, and at the height of the flood the water was within three or four feet of the crown of the arch. Beyond the tunnel this tremendous volume met another cascade, coming down the hillside as over a weir, and the wild confluence of waters caused the most spectacular breach of all; for a huge slice of the hillside, and the railway with it, slid down into the deep glen of the Pease Burn. Burn indeed! That afternoon it was more like a small Niagara. The mercy of the whole affair was that at the time the catastrophe occurred there was not a single train on either line in the twenty-eight miles between Berwick and Dunbar. Half an hour later there would have been eight or nine, and what the death roll might have been does not bear thinking about.

The adventures of the four northbound expresses diverted at Newcastle were by no means over when they were turned on to the cross-country line via Carlisle, because by Galashiels they were coming into the Lammermuir disaster zone. The 9.50 a.m. from King's Cross was leading the way but, although Gala Water was flooded and there were trails of destruction everywhere, the railway, awash in several places, was still intact and this train managed to get through, over the summit at Falahill, and safely down into Edinburgh. As for the second train, the 10.5 a.m. to Aberdeen, the situation was best summed up as told me by the Scottish Region Locomotive Superintendent who by that time was in the Control Office at Edinburgh. They had a telephone call from the driver, I think it was from Tynehead; standing at the telephone on the signal post he was up to his waist in water, and reported a deeper flood ahead and what looked like a landslip. There was nothing for it but to order him back to Carlisle and hope the LMS line could take them over Beattock and by the old Caledonian way into Edinburgh.

Worst hit of all was the Flying Scotsman, by that time nearing Hawick, and now turned back for the second time. Fourth to leave London, and third in the cavalcade that had been diverted west from Newcastle, was the Queen of Scots Pullman. By the time the Aberdeen express had run into the floods at Tynehead the Pullman had reached Galashiels; she also was ordered back to Carlisle and, as her eventual destination was Glasgow, Control decided to send her direct by the LMS line, transferring her Edinburgh passengers to other trains. The Flying Scotsman eventually crept into Edinburgh at 3.51 a.m., all but ten hours late.

The ultimate toll of this apocalyptic afternoon was the London–Edinburgh main line completely breached in *nine* places, seven bridges destroyed, and three major landslips. In addition to all this, and apart from many cases of lesser damage, there was that critical embankment—'Ayton Dam', as it became known—but not a single life lost on the railway. When the full extent of the damage had been revealed, and much of it could be reached only by lengthy walking, the civil engineers did not expect the line to be open again for at least six months, and while reconstruction work was in progress arrangements for working the traffic had to be made. From the viewpoint of locomotive operating the simplest and perhaps the quickest route between Edinburgh and Newcastle would have been via Carlisle. But in passenger business alone there were many trains by day and night, and added to all the regular traffic there it would have been very difficult to arrange all the necessary paths, as well as for the servicing of locomotives. On the other hand among the precautions taken against possible wartime damage another alternative route was immediately available. The majestic Royal Border Bridge built by Robert Stephenson, by which the East Coast main line crosses the Tweed and enters Berwick, lies perilously near to the sea; and a well-aimed shot from a coastal raider, or a single bomb striking one of the immensely tall piers, could have breached the main line for as long as the cloudburst of August 1948 did in peacetime. Such a mischance had to be guarded against.

From Tweedmouth Junction, just south of the Royal Border Bridge, a branch line ran up the valley of the Tweed. It was built as early as 1849 by the then York, Newcastle and Berwick Railway, intending to reach Kelso. But in the exciting game of railway politics played with such gusto in mid-Victorian times, its progress was blocked by an advance of the North British Railway from the west, and the two railways ended up just one mile apart, at Spronston and Mellendean Burn, the former 20 miles from Tweedmouth Junction. The link-up was made two years later, and it was this line, with its continuation through Kelso and Roxburgh to its junction with the Waverley Route near St Boswells, that was scheduled as an alternative main line between Newcastle and Edinburgh. Although originally of no more than branch line status and including a great deal of tiresome curvature, it was substantially upgraded and, what was more important, authorized to take the largest passenger and freight locomotives, though at much restricted speed. Over the 22¼ miles from Tweedmouth to Kelso speed was limited to 45 m.p.h., and from there onwards to the junction near St Boswells no more than 25 m.p.h. was permitted with the big engines. Such a restriction, however, was nothing to the inconvenience that could have been caused if 'Pacific' engines had been banned, so as to involve engine changing at Tweedmouth and inevitable double-heading afterwards, with the heavy trains.

So while this route was not required at any time during the war, it was brought into use as part of the London–Edinburgh main line for nearly three months in 1948. It was indeed a fascinating experience to ride over it on the footplate, and on no less a train than the Flying Scotsman. It was on a raw autumnal day in late October 1948 that I made my trip. The 'non-stop' service between Edinburgh and London was no longer operating, and the first passenger stop was at Newcastle; but on this 'emergency' route several other stops were needed, with a heavy train of about 510 tons. Our engine was one of the Gresley Class 'A4' streamlined 'Pacifics', No. 60027 *Merlin*, one of the crack No. 1 link at Haymarket, the duties of which included the running of the 'non-stop' to London during the summer season; and it needed the élitest of élite among engines to hold that job down. It was not merely a case of free steaming and plenty of power to pull in the cylinders: there was a need for faultless mechanical performance, particularly in lubrication. All the Haymarket No. 1 link engines had their own regular crews, and normally no others—two crews to an engine—and this instilled a spirit of ownership and a special pride in the job. But the disaster of August 1948 and the emergency route workings caused much derangement, and when I rode *Merlin* things were far from normal. As it happened she did have one of her regular crews, but she had been in common-user duty and was not in the immaculate condition that one ordinarily expected in that link.

*Merlin* was a locomotive with a name the significance of which could be misinterpreted. She was actually one of a series named after the swiftest birds of the air, of which *Golden Eagle* and the immortal *Mallard* were others. By a coincidence, during the war a group of Southern Railway 4–6–0s of the 'King Arthur' class, lent to the LNER and working mostly north of Newcastle, included one also named *Merlin*, but in that case the name referred to the magician of the Arthurian legend. But to Scottish railwaymen the *Merlin* I rode had an association different from both swift birds and magicians. In Fife, beside the Edinburgh–Dundee main line over which the engine regularly worked, was a Naval shore base, 'H.M.S. Merlin', and the staff there unofficially 'adopted' engine No. 60027, to the extent that a decorative plaque was presented to the LNER and carried with pride on the streamlined flanks of the engine. Our big load was well above the limit, even for such fine engines as the 'A4s', on the long 1 in 70 ascent from Hardengreen Junction to Falahill summit, and we stopped to take a bank engine in rear. This was one of the powerful North British 'Glen' class 4–4–0s and even with two such engines as an 'A4' and one of these 'Glens' we could not do more than 22 to 25 m.p.h. on this toilsome incline. The first 18 miles from Edinburgh up to Falahill took 41¾ minutes.

Then we had an easy run down to Galashiels, but with none of the speed for which the 'A4s' are famed. The curves are incessant, and only at a few points was speed allowed to rise to about 60 m.p.h. At Galashiels we stopped to take water. On the Waverley route there is no stretch level enough to permit of any such aid to long distance running as water troughs. While water was being taken the driver took the opportunity to go round the engine, and found to his concern that the right-hand driving axlebox was a good deal warmer than it should have been. No substitute engine was available and, with the agreement of a senior locomotive officer who was riding with us, he decided to make a run for Tweedmouth; it was taking a risk, but with the continuous slow running after St Boswells, no undue load would be put upon that bearing. At the same time word was sent ahead to Tweedmouth shed to have a relief engine ready to take over. The driver was very upset to think that 'his engine' was likely to become a casualty; and although our 25 m.p.h. crawl from St Boswells to Kelso, and the subsequent 'drift' at 45 m.p.h., did not exert the engine in the slightest we rode into Tweedmouth with *flames* coming out of that axlebox. We were on time nevertheless, and the senior officer remarked laconically 'I'm afraid we've jiggered that bearing.' The driver was not so polite, and said with some vehemence 'This would *never* have happened if we'd had regular charge of her'.

My railway friends took me back to Edinburgh by the coast road so that I could see the almost completed temporary bridges that had been built so that the line could be opened for traffic. Trains were actually running again on some parts of the route, and it was a marvellous feat of organization to have the line open again, albeit at much reduced speed, in less than three months after that fearful cloudburst. This was the first railway to cross the Border, the line from Edinburgh to Berwick, which from its very beginning in 1844 took the resounding title of North British Railway. But nothing in its long history can compare with that cataclysm of nature during those few hours in the afternoon of 12 August 1948.

# 5 Engine Testing

During my early training at Imperial College I learned the art of engine testing. Apart from the disciplined reading of pressure gauges, dials, and other measuring instruments, there was the fascinating but tricky job of 'indicating'—the taking of indicator diagrams, those vital loops, something like the shape of a man's boot, that, suitably measured, tell you the power being developed in the cylinders. The paper on which the diagram was drawn was carried on a small cylinder, about an inch in diameter, and 2 in. long, which was rotated on its axis first one way and then the other, in synchronization with the movement of the piston in the cylinder to be indicated. The pencil of the apparatus was mounted on a linkage actuated up and down according to the rise and fall of pressure in the cylinder. It needed plenty of practice and a light touch to apply that pencil to the rapidly moving paper, and with steam or oil about most of us only succeeded in tearing the paper at our first attempts. But in due course I indicated simple and compound steam engines, small gas and oil engines, and a diesel. I still have in my old college notebooks some of the diagrams I took.

It is one thing, however, to indicate engines in the rarefied atmosphere of a college laboratory, quite another to deal with a steam locomotive at speed. The indicator has to be fixed close to the cylinders, which on most locomotives were far away from any shelter. At the Institution of Mechanical Engineers I met fellow students who were undergoing training at one or another of the principal railway works, and I learned how temporary shelters were built round the front of locomotives to be tested, in which men would take the indicator diagrams and read the temperature gauges. The challenge of such experimental work, in the rough and tumble of express running, out on the front of a swaying and pitching engine at 60 to 70 m.p.h., fairly captured my imagination, and I hoped that one day the technique I had learned at college might be put to use on a locomotive. In the magnificent library at South Kensington I sought out every scrap of information I could find on testing, and as a student of the Institution of Mechanical Engineers I had access to past issues of the Proceedings. But after I had graduated and done a further year of postgraduate studies the opportunities then existing for entering upon a career in engineering led me into different ways, and it was not until my literary work had developed that I began to enter the charmed circle of steam locomotive testing.

Many years before that, however, another facet of my practical work at college stood me in good stead on two occasions when I was riding on the footplate. We tested a Lancashire boiler. This was a stationary power-station job, and although our main task was to make a scientific record of its steam-raising capacity, it was a tradition that we should all take turns in firing it. Now for a novice a Lancashire boiler is not the easiest thing to fire. The door is about four feet above the ground, and one had to swing the shovel so that the coal was spread evenly over the long, flat grate. Some of my fellow students, particularly those who in that era came to college immaculately dressed, fought shy of this job, with laughable results. Fortunately the stalwart laboratory assistant was there to keep boiler pressure up when these rather unwilling 'firemen' were on the job. But I must say I revelled in it, once I had got the hang of swinging the shovel.

Then, one day about ten years after leaving college, I was making a round trip from Marylebone to Sheffield and back on the footplate. For some special observations I had been asked to go down on the early morning newspaper train leaving London at 2.32 a.m., and the return journey was by way of a bonus. At Leicester, the Great Northern 'Atlantic' which I had ridden from Sheffield was replaced by a new 4–6–0 of the 'Sandringham' class, in charge of two of the most carefree enginemen I have ever travelled with. We had not gone far before I sensed they were out to pull my leg. I had been up since 1 a.m. and in other circumstances would have been glad to go back into the train and get my head down; but this new driver and his mate were irresistible. The opening run from Leicester to Woodford was uneventful; then, when we got the 'right away', the driver shouted across 'Quick, open the regulator', and left me to start the engine. The 'Sandringhams', like all the later Gresley engines, had a regulator valve that was operated from a horizontal rod extending across the backplate of the firebox, with a pull-out handle at both ends. I seized the handle on the fireman's side and with two hefty tugs pulled it fully out, and away we went.

Then it was the fireman's turn. After putting a bit on, he turned to me saying 'Well, come on', and handed me the shovel. The engine was then accelerating rapidly, and was jazzing about in the style characteristic of her class. For a moment I was staggering a bit, to their amusement; and when, just as I was swinging the shovel, the engine made a lurch and I missed the firedoor completely and scattered a whole shovelful of coal all over the footplate, they laughed their heads off. But I soon got my 'sea legs', and found this engine a good deal easier to fire than that Lancashire boiler at college; for about twenty minutes or so I gave the driver all the steam he needed. Their leg-pulling continued, but more in the spirit of being 'brothers in overalls' than of ragging the visitor!

The second occasion on which I fired an express was not so funny. I had a pass to ride the engine of the Highland Mail from Perth to Inverness. It was mid-winter, before dawn, in bitterly cold weather. The train leaving at 6.25 a.m. was very heavy, nearly 500 tons, and our engine, one of the then brand new 'Black Five' 4–6–0s, had one of the Horwich 2–6–0 'Crabs'—so called because of the curious look of their outside Walschaerts valve gear—to assist her over the Grampians. With two engines the earlier part of the run was easy work, and up the level stretch of Strathtay, north of Dunkeld, we were bowling along at over 50 m.p.h. On the train engine we had another task. As far as Blair Atholl the line is single-tracked and our driver was responsible for exchanging the tablets at each crossing loop. In British single line working at that time signals were not enough; possession of a tablet exclusive to the section was the ultimate authority to proceed. On the Highland Railway the crossing places were equipped with apparatus for mechanical tablet exchange, in connection with complementary apparatus on the locomotives; so that whereas on lines not so furnished trains had to slow down to 20 m.p.h. or so, to enable signalmen and firemen to exchange by hand, on the Highland it was often done at 60 m.p.h. After such an exchange the driver had to lean out from the cab, take the tablet just collected and check it was for the right section of line, and then place it in the delivery arm ready for discharge at the next crossing loop.

This operation had, of course, to be done by night as well as by day. It is always a matter for amazement to railwaymen from countries outside Europe that we have never used headlights on British locomotives. In Great Britain, however, with all railways continuously fenced, even on the most lonely and desolate sections, the need was never felt for any form of headlight, and on the contrary the small oil lamps carried were so disposed as to indicate the class of train. Up in the Highlands of Scotland, where there were many lonely stretches without a single habitation for ten miles or more, the experienced drivers seemed to develop a sixth sense, of locality. I shall always remember one being introduced to me at Fort William, with the words 'he could find his way to Mallaig blindfold'.

It was still pitch dark when we left Perth on that cold January morning, and our driver was carrying out the tablet-exchanging work with precision; but on this train there was a second exchanging function at some stations, that performed by the travelling post office. Mail bags had to be set down and picked up at full speed by the traductor apparatus on the van and the lineside standards and nets. I shall have more to tell of work in the TPO in my next chapter, but now I come to the incident that led to my taking the shovel. We were nearing Ballinluig at nearly 60 m.p.h. There came the usual 'wham' as we delivered one tablet and picked up the one for the next section. Reading my watch by the light from the fire I noted that we had taken 31½ minutes to cover the 23½ miles from Perth, and then, looking up after noting down the time, I was horrified to see the driver, capless, slumping down over the controls. The fireman sounded the alarm code on the whistle and made an emergency application of the brake.

We had hardly stopped before the driver of the leading engine was in the cab, and between us we lifted the dazed driver over to the seat on the right hand side, where I had been. He had caught his head on the mailbag hanging on the lineside standard, and at the speed we were going it had naturally stunned him—fortunately not seriously. Few words were spoken. The driver of the leading engine said to me 'You can put some fire on', and returned to his own engine. I see from my notes, made at the time, that we were standing for no more than 75 *seconds*, and proceeded on our way with the fireman driving and myself firing. It was less than twelve miles to Blair Atholl, and from the shed there we could get a relief engineman. I did not have to fire for long. We made an extra, though brief, stop at Pitlochry station, and as we were pounding our way up into the Pass of Killiecrankie, and I had already forgotten what a cold morning it was, the driver rallied sufficiently to get up from the seat, cross to the left hand side once more and take over. Talk about 'guts'! No relief was asked for at Blair Atholl, and he completed his rostered duty right through to Inverness. He kept time too, despite the extra stop at Pitlochry and the emergency stop north of Ballinluig.

Shortly after the end of the Second World War in 1946, a firm that I had hitherto associated with bookselling rather than publishing wrote to say that, in view of the impending nationalization of the railways, they were proposing to publish four books each dealing with one of the 'Big Four', and inviting me to do the one on the Great Western. They mentioned other authors who were being asked to do the remaining three books, but in the event mine was the only one of the four that actually got off the ground. The Great Western gave me virtually the freedom of the line, and when the time came to visit Swindon works it could not have been more fortunate, because some scientific trials were being made on a locomotive of the 'King' class, and I was invited to see some of these in progress on the stationary testing plant in the works. Until that time it had been generally understood that this plant at Swindon was of no more than limited capacity. It had been installed by the great G. J. Churchward some forty years earlier; but in the period between the two world wars it had been little used. All the important testing of that time had been done out on the road, with the dynamometer car. In the late 1930s however the plant had been completely rebuilt, and was now able to absorb the maximum power output of the latest and largest locomotives.

I shall never forget my first sight of the plant in action. To maintain the standard of pre-war performance, with post-war quality coal, F. W. Hawksworth, the Chief Mechanical Engineer, was trying out some important alterations to the boilers of various classes of locomotive, and here was the *King Edward III* being put through his paces in most thrilling style. The engine was securely anchored at the cab end, and each of the coupled wheels rested on a carrier wheel, in the same way as exhibition working models are mounted in their glass cases, except that the operation is reversed. The real locomotive drove the carrier wheels, and brakes were applied hydraulically to the axles of these carrier wheels, so that the power needed to drive them was equal to that needed to haul a loaded train on the road. By careful adjustment the speed could be held steady for an hour or more. On my first visit to the test plant the *King Edward III* was running at 'sixty miles per hour'—at least the wheels were revolving at the corresponding speed—and 'hauling' the equivalent of a twenty-coach train. It was tremendous, and I took a little time to absorb fully the details of what was going on.

I was fortunate in having Sam Ell as my guide and mentor; for no more dedicated and skilled engineer has ever tested steam locomotives. Although a Great Western man to his fingertips, he was broadminded and ready enough to extol the merits of other designs, which was more than could be said of some of his contemporaries elsewhere in Great Britain. From his apprenticeship in Swindon Works Ell had graduated through the Drawing Office, and became attached to the experimental section. He worked under such fine testing specialists as W. H. Pearce and Conrad K. Dumas, when the first 'Castle' class engines were built. Then in the 1930s he was associated with C. T. Roberts, in a junior capacity, when that distinguished engineer was feeling his way towards the principle that later became known as Controlled Road Testing and was adopted as standard practice by the nationalized British Railways. In 1947 when I first met him, Ell was already in charge of experimental testing on the Great Western Railway.

Coming back to the *King Edward III*, the performance was being examined just as though it was a stationary engine in a laboratory. Men were taking indicator diagrams and reading the numerous gauges, while on the footplate the driver and fireman were at work just as if they were out on the road—or nearly the same. The driver's main task was so to adjust the controls as to keep the speed steady at 60 m.p.h. against the load that was being applied through the carrying wheels beneath, while, so that a close check could be kept on the rate of firing, the coal had been made up into weighed bags containing one hundredweight each and, as these were delivered to the shovelling plate and emptied, the time was noted down. Above all, for me, there was the experience of being able to walk along the gallery beside the engine, within a few feet of the swiftly revolving wheels and the pistons and connecting rods. At 60 m.p.h. the engine was making 268 revolutions per minute, more than twice as fast as those stationary engines I had tested at college, and the men taking indicator cards were experts. There were no torn cards!

There is naturally a great difference between engine testing on a stationary plant such as this, where all the conditions can be closely controlled, and road tests with the dynamometer car, on which one is subject to the exigencies of traffic, even though the dynamometer car may be attached to a special test train. Numerous extraneous factors enter into it to affect the overall performance of the locomotive. There is the variation in speed, in gradient, and the likely incidence of checks from adverse signals, or the need to slow down because of civil engineering work on the line. Above all there is the effect of variable weather conditions. One might imagine that when one came to check up, and related the coal and water consumption to the actual work done as precisely measured in the dynamometer car, the variables would equalize out—if less work had been done, less coal would have been burned, and so on. But this is not necessarily the case, and is in fact very rarely so. On a series of six tests carried out on one of the LNER 'Pacific' engines between Doncaster and King's Cross there was a 20 per cent variation between the maximum and minimum recordings of coal consumption in relation to the total amount of work done on the drawbar, measured in horsepower hours.

At the same time as these first post-war tests were in progress on the Great Western Railway a momentous development was in hand on the LMS. To secure the advantages of testing at constant speed without the necessity of withdrawing a locomotive from traffic for considerable periods and running it on a stationary plant, a mobile laboratory was designed by Dr H. I. Andrews of the research department at Derby, which, by a brilliantly ingenious system of electric loading, enabled a locomotive to be run at constant speed over a line of fluctuating gradients. When it was travelling uphill the load on the drawbar was automatically lessened, as it was correspondingly increased when the running was downhill. With the use of two of the so-called Mobile Test Units, and a dynamometer, the traction effect of a train of fifteen coaches or more could be simulated. I had the pleasure and privilege of travelling with Dr Andrews when, after nationalization, he was making tests on one of the 'Merchant Navy' class 'Pacifics' on the Southern Region, and we ran from London to Salisbury and back. The constant speed stipulated was to be 50 m.p.h., but in tests of this kind, 'out the line', care has to be taken in the timetable planning, because many trains would be travelling a great deal faster on some sections.

On the outward journey we were to follow after the Atlantic Coast Express had gone through. To secure the necessary platform occupancy for all the preliminaries the test train was started from one of the 'Windsor Lines' platforms at Clapham Junction, and proceeded, not under test conditions, down the 'Riverside' line as far as Point Pleasant Junction, and then took the spur that led us soon to Wimbledon, where the West of England main line was joined. So, with that huge 'airsmoothed' 'Pacific' engine, and only the three test vehicles, we followed the Atlantic Coast Express, and the test proper began at Esher, 50 m.p.h. unvarying without a break for the 52 miles onwards to Andover. It was extraordinary to see how precisely the speed was held, irrespective of the gradients, because other stipulated features of the test were a completely unchanged rate of admission of steam to the cylinders, and a constant pressure, not necessarily in the boiler but in the steam chest just before entry into the cylinders. The automatic controls adjusted the load so that the cylinders could run the test train at 50 m.p.h. regardless of all extraneous conditions. This running at constant speed sometimes caused astonishment to men working on the line. The stipulated test speeds were not always as high as 50 m.p.h. On one occasion, ordinary testing being finished, some high power readings at no more than 20 m.p.h. were required. The engine pounded along making a tremendous noise from the exhaust, downhill, with only three coaches, and some platelayers stood reverently at the lineside, and doffed their caps as the 'funeral' went by!

In view of my own earlier experiences the taking of indicator diagrams on this train was of exceptional interest. It would in any case have been impossible to have erected a shelter round the front of this totally encased locomotive; but the diagrams were taken on an indicator mounted in the dynamometer car, and actuated by remote control. The indicator was one of a type used by the Royal Aircraft Establishment at Farnborough in the testing of aero-engines. In a separate compartment in the dynamometer car I was able to watch the taking of the diagrams at close range, with a sophistication far removed from the procedure I had learned, and which I saw being used at Swindon. This however is not to say that the Mobile Test Unit of Dr Andrews has proved the last word in steam locomotive testing. It certainly got over the problems of variable speed and variable effort present in road testing of locomotives. It was doing laboratory work on the track; but by that time in British railway history there was arising a strong conviction that constant speed testing was not enough. Neither was the old fashioned practice of just measuring horsepower, coal and water consumption on an ordinary service train. From the work of C. T. Roberts with the Great Western dynamometer car in the 1930s a new principle was presented and accepted as the future standard by the nationalized British Railways. Its first exponent was Sam Ell.

In the 1930s the Great Western testing staff had found that many of the point-to-point timings of express trains were unrealistic, in respect of loads and locomotive power, and Ell set out to translate the test results obtained first on the stationary plant at Swindon into a practical guide whereby train timings could be established with a reasonable certainty of their being kept. Careful analysis of many hundreds of recordings, not only in the dynamometer car but also in published logs in the *Railway Magazine*, had shown generally that on those occasions when a maximum effort was being made, the performance corresponded roughly to a constant rate of steaming.

The desirability of a constant steam rate on a locomotive can be compared in a familiar way to the performance of an ordinary motor car. All drivers know that they get a much more efficient performance on a long run, in terms of miles per gallon, when the car is running for hours on end with little in the way of interruption; and that the petrol consumption becomes much heavier in what might be called ‘taxi work’. So it was with steam locomotives. If one could run so that the rate of firing coal and production of steam was fairly steady, one secured a much more efficient performance than if the run was a series of ‘fits and starts’. A good driver would always endeavour to keep things as steady as he could.

Runs on the test plant were of course made at a precisely constant rate, and at constant speed as well; but these maximum-effort runs, most of them in ordinary service when the driver and fireman did not know that a detailed record was being made of their work, showed every sign that the steam rate was fairly constant, although the speed would be varying a good deal, uphill and down dale. I was surprised and delighted to learn from Ell that many of the logs I had compiled purely for my own interest, and which had been subsequently published in Cecil J. Allen's monthly articles in the *Railway Magazine*, had been subjected to searching analysis at Swindon!

This work provided convincing evidence that it was not unrealistic to run service express passenger trains at constant rates of steaming, and that this was likely to yield the most economical use of fuel. The next step was to devise an instrument to assist the driver—not in ordinary service, but on a series of dynamometer test runs made in many parts of the country. A test would be stipulated at, for example, a constant evaporation rate of 20,000 lbs of steam per hour, and from previous data a load would be made up so that this steam rate would give a speed of 60 m.p.h. on level track. The speed might be 45 or 50 m.p.h. uphill, and 75 to 80 m.p.h. downhill, but it was the driver's task to adjust the controls so that the steam rate did not vary. To help him do so an instrument like a thermometer in the form of a U was fixed just in front of him, in his corner of the cab, and this gadget was graduated so that certain marks on the tube corresponded to definite steam rates. He had to keep the mercury column on the specified mark.

This method of testing proved extraordinarily successful, and provided the outstandingly important result that coal and water consumptions at a certain steam rate were the same on a variable speed run out on the line, as on a run at constant speed on one of the testing plants, either at Swindon or on the new one at Rugby. Of course there was a limit to the routes over which the 'Controlled Road' system of testing could be applied. On the London Midland Region the far-famed Settle and Carlisle route was used, and there one could work at a constant steam rate on the ascent from the north to Aisgill summit. There are plenty of variable gradients on the way; but the tests had to be concluded shortly after passing Aisgill, because on the steep descent to Settle the speed would have risen much too high.

I must conclude with the tale of an amusing contretemps, before testing became the highly disciplined business that it became in the 1950s. In earlier LMS days one of the Stanier 4–6–0 engines was being tested between Carlisle and Crewe. Men were indicating out on the front and the old Lancashire and Yorkshire Railway dynamometer car was in use. A young and rather inexperienced engineer had been posted observer on the footplate and, to ensure that good 'fat' diagrams were obtained, the man in charge in the dynamometer car told him to be sure the driver kept the regulator full open while diagrams were being taken. Well, they pounded their way from Carlisle, and in due course topped Shap Summit. The descent to Carnforth was usually made under easy steam, and few if any indicator cards were taken. The novice on the footplate did not know this, and when the driver began easing the regulator back he intervened at once, shouting 'No—keep it full open.' The driver muttered something about 'going too bloody fast', but orders were orders, and they were soon descending the 1 in 75 gradient of Shap like a veritable thunderbolt—still with the regulator full open! Fortunately the line is dead straight; but when those in the dynamometer car saw the speedometer needle pass the 80 mark, then 85, 90, and 95 m.p.h., it was time to put the 'intercom' into operation and ask just what the hell was going on!

# 6 Newspapers—Bankers—Posts

Around the turn of the century the launching of two great enterprises almost coincided. These were the opening of the London extension of the Great Central Railway, to the new terminus at Marylebone, and the birth of the *Daily Mail* newspaper. Almost at once a special train was chartered to take the newspaper to its distribution centres in the Midlands. It left Marylebone at 2.45 a.m., serving Brackley, Rugby, Leicester, Nottingham and Sheffield, and was at first exclusive to the *Daily Mail*; later it was made available to other newspapers, but not until some time afterwards did it convey ordinary passengers, and then only to the extent of a single coach. In the 1930s it was the fastest newspaper train in the world, and the departure time was 2.32 a.m. The LNER were very proud of this train, and were somewhat nettled when in 1933–4 the Great Western indulged in a little publicity for their newly-introduced South Wales newspaper train, which *they* claimed as the fastest in the world. The latter train certainly made a good run from Paddington to Newport, 133½ miles in 137 minutes, at a start-to-stop average of 58½ m.p.h.; but the Great Central train had three successive sections at 59.7, 59.8 and 61.5 m.p.h., in each case start-to-stop.

One morning my friend E. G. Marsden, then Information Agent of the LNER, rang up and asked me to call on him. 'I'm annoyed about the publicity that has been given to this Great Western newspaper train,' he said, 'and I want to take a rise out of them.' He went on to emphasize that they, the Eastern group, had been running a very fast newspaper train for over thirty years, and I remember breaking in and saying 'Yes, and one that demands far harder locomotive work, and much higher maximum speeds than this new Great Western train.' He then asked if I would like to ride down on the footplate one morning and write up my experiences, adding, almost apologetically, 'I'm afraid if you do, you'll have a rather grisly night!' But I was then forty years younger than I am now, and I jumped at the opportunity. With a start at that hour in the morning there was no point in going to bed at all. I caught the last electric train up from Bushey to Euston, had a snack at an all-night coffee stall, and got to Marylebone about 1.30 a.m. to watch the arrival of newspapers still damp from the presses, and their loading into the train.

H. V. Morton once described Marylebone as 'the one London station that is not entirely hideous' (shades of Brunel, and his majestic creation at Paddington!), but at that hour in the morning Marylebone was astonishingly far removed from its usual Cathedral close like atmosphere. Van after van came tearing in from Fleet Street, and it was not long before some of the eight vans of the train were stacked almost to their roofs. Soon after 2 a.m. the engine came backing down, bringing for me the one disappointment of the trip. From the driver and fireman I learned that the regular engines on the job were the former Great Central four-cylinder 4–6–0s of the 'Lord Faringdon' class, massive things first introduced in 1918, by John G. Robinson. Though not always at their best in heavy load haulage, they were very fast runners, and ideal for the 'Newspaper'. But the object of my trip was to provide an exposition of LNER prowess, and it was deemed necessary to use a new standard, rather than a pre-grouping engine. So we had a Gresley three-cylinder 4–6–0 of the 'Sandringham' class, the *Gayton Hill.* She proved a splendid engine in every way, though a slight disappointment in that I missed the only opportunity that might have come my way of riding on a true Great Central locomotive.

Two-thirty a.m.! A last van dashed into the station. Papers were loaded like lightning, and a door slammed. Far down the platform a green light shone, and we were right away. At first, except that there were no other trains about, the run began like any other journey after dark; but as we stormed out through the sleeping suburbs of London there were fewer and fewer lights and, once we were round the curve at Rickmansworth and climbing into the Chilterns, the night was of a pitch darkness I had not previously experienced on the footplate. The glare from the open fire door lit up the beech woods through which we were passing; all the stations were in darkness, and only the heavy beat of the engine told me we were climbing a steep gradient. Then, once we topped the crest of the hills at Amersham, the pace became thrilling beyond description.

I had long previously learned to measure train speeds off the beat of the wheels over the rail joints—the noise that the child of immortal memory once called the 'diddly-da's'. But it is not always possible to do that on a locomotive, among all the metallic bangs and clatters of normal running. Our engine on the 'Newspaper' was fairly good, however, and I had no difficulty; and just now we were tearing down into the Vale of Aylesbury. The summer night was still pitch black: not a glimmer of light from the surrounding countryside, signals few and far between, and here we were hurtling downhill at 85 m.p.h. A scream on the whistle to warn anyone who was about at Aylesbury we were coming, and then round the curve, 'whoosh', we were through and out again into the blackness of the night. On now, on to a more gently undulating track till we reached our first stop, Brackley, 59¼ miles in 64¾ minutes—two minutes early.

Harder still on the next stage, with the first signs of dawn. Not a word spoken between us. The fireman stoking assiduously, the driver constantly looking out. Up through Woodford, into Catesby Tunnel, where water is always dripping and the cab glasses became spattered as with rain. A headlong dash down to Braunston, at 84 m.p.h., and so into Rugby—just *fourteen seconds* inside booked time. It was practically daylight as we got away for *Gayton Hall*'s last stage, the 19.9 mile run to Leicester. There was some stiff climbing up from Rugby to Ashby Magna, but on the last length the driver gave this noble engine her head, and on a straight and splendid piece of track the speed swept up to a full 90 m.p.h. With every justification the LNER could claim that *theirs* was the fastest newspaper train in the world. At this high speed the engine rode well, and with the usual breathless finish into Leicester, traditional for thirty years on the Great Central, we arrived a minute early. That our gains on time were so small was indeed a testimony to the sharpness of the schedule.

At Leicester we exchanged *Gayton Hall* for one of the latest 'Sandringham' class engines named after football clubs, in this case *Derby County*, and in one version of the article I subsequently wrote, published in one of the *Daily Mail* group of newspapers, the subeditor evidently got a bit confused between footplates and footballs. He put a subheading to the article 'Sandringhams provide foot*ball* thrills'! Be that as it may, *Derby County* continued to feast me with exciting and valuable data. At Nottingham the newspapers were unloaded at Arkwright Street station, on a viaduct, and the bundles sent down chutes to where the delivery vans were waiting at street level below. This proved the fastest lap of all, because the 22.6 miles from Leicester were covered in 21¼ minutes start-to-stop, an average of 64 m.p.h. In such haste were the newspapers taken from London to the Midlands in the 1930s.

Deep in the West Midlands is one of the greatest curiosities of British railway topography, the Lickey Incline. One of the early lines, the Birmingham and Gloucester was finely engineered with a freedom from curves and easy gradients, except in one place. The range of the Lickey Hills lay exactly athwart the line of route, and instead of making a detour or using any other artifice to ease the gradient, the original engineer took his track clean over a precipice,

1 Live steam at Reading: 1908

2 Slide-rule pushing in the top floor 'den', Bushey, 1936

3 Train photography with a Box-Brownie, 1920: a northbound train on the Furness Railway near Thwaite Flat Junction (between Barrow and Askam) hauled by a Pettigrew '130' class 4–4–0

4 The southbound Highland Mail leaving Aviemore, in 1928, hauled by one of the 'River' class 4–6–0s, then painted in Midland red

5 The Royal Scot express climbing Shap in a gale of wind, in 1931, before smoke-deflecting plates had been added to these locomotives

6 The *Cock o' the North*, LNER, on its early trials in 1934, here seen at Peterborough, with indicator shelters at the front end, other test equipment, and the dynamometer car coupled behind the tender

7 The Coronation Scot safely back in Euston, after the dramatic demonstration run to Crewe and back on 29 June 1937, when a maximum speed of 114 m.p.h. was claimed

8 E. C. Bredin's beautiful Irish 4–6–0 *Maeve* ready to leave Cork with the English Mail: Driver Foley, Inspector Murphy, Fireman Ryan about to be joined by the author on the footplate

9 On the footplate in 1944: the GWR 4–6–0 *Usk Castle* during the brief station stop at Exeter on the morning express from Plymouth to Liverpool and Manchester

10 On one of the first LNER 'B1' 4–6–0s in 1945: working from Ipswich to March, with Driver Sansom and Fireman Norris, of Ipswich depot

11 Ben Nevis, seen from the footplate of a 'K2' 2–6–0 leaving Banavie for Fort William in 1946

12 On the first high-superheat 'King' in 1949, ready to leave Paddington with the 3.30 p.m. to Plymouth; Fireman Preston, Inspector Pullen, Driver Angel on the footplate

13 Youthful enginemen: with Driver Stokes and Fireman Davis, whose ages did not add up to mine, on the Lickey 0–10–0 bank engine No. 58100 'Big Bertha', in 1949

14 Night mail from Paddington in 1952: on the 'Star' class engine No. 4062 *Malmesbury Abbey* with the Penzance Postal Special with left to right, Inspector Davies, Fireman Howlett and Driver Hares

15 The rejuvenated *City of Truro* at Kingswear, in 1957. On this trip, when running non-stop from Teignmouth to Bristol, the engine attained 84 m.p.h. Note: the tank engine assisted only over the very heavy gradients of the branch line as far as Newton Abbot

16 Conversation piece at Hullavington in 1954: a chat with the stationmaster and photographer P. M. Alexander

17 Gresley A3s on the Midland: at Leeds in 1960 ready to ride *The White Knight* to Carlisle, with Driver Waite, Inspector Pullan, and Fireman Gibson

18 Northallerton new power box, in 1939: hauling the control panel up to the top floor

19 Engineers on the job: installing the new type of marshalling yard retarder at Perth, in 1960; my colleagues Eric Harris and Gordon Todhunter fitting the strain gauges prior to full load trials

20 South Africa, 1968: with A. H. Croxton (formerly Operating Superintendent, Rhodesia Railways) and J. T. Barnard (Divisional Mechanical Engineer, Cape Town) at Paarden Eiland motive power depot, near Cape Town

21 On the footplate of a 'GEA' class Beyer-Garratt locomotive riding from Mossel Bay to George, Cape Province

22 The 'charge' up the coal loading gallery, at Port Elizabeth, with one of the big '15F' 4–8–2s in the foreground

23 Concentration! Driving the *King George V* tender first round the Bulmer circuit at Hereford in June 1969

24 On a vintage caboose in Canada in 1971

25 Tournai, Belgium, 1969, in the Art Gallery: as President of the Institution of Railway Signal Engineers replying (in French) to the speech of welcome by the Burgomaster. Seated in the front row, next to Olivia, my wife, is M. Louis Devillers, Director of Electrical Engineering and Signalling on the Belgian National Railways

26 Heavy freight in the Canadian Rockies: climbing the Field Hill, British Columbia, with four diesel locomotives, on a spectacular spiral location.

27 Seconds later, the head end of the train crosses its own tail as the rearmost cars approach the lower end of the spiral tunnel

28 One of the passenger diesel locomotives of the Canadian Pacific: climbing aboard for a run on the Montreal commuter service

29 The 'snapper' snapped! An extraordinary grade crossing in Vermont, USA, where even in 1971 ancient high-ball signals protect a sparsely used crossing of the Maine Central and Central Vermont Railroads

30 Zero weather on the Algoma Central in 1974: after shunting at Franz, Ontario, where the Canadian Pacific main line is intersected, the snow-plastered diesels back down to re-couple to our train

31 The vintage 'Prairie Dog Central' train out on the prairies west of Winnipeg, in August 1971

32 Complete with Japanese 'steaming hat' (two sizes too small!) on a 'C57' class 'Pacific' ready to work a freight train south from Miyazaki, island of Kyushu, in 1973

33 Inspection trolley—four manpower—at Lonavla, summit of the Bhor Ghat, on the Central Railway of India main line from Bombay to Poona, in 1975

34 Sixty years on: from school at Giggleswick (1916) to preparations for the Settle and Carlisle Centenary (1976): with Alex Murray, PRO of the London Midland Region at Aisgill summit, 1975

35 Doing the 'ton' on the cushions: on the engineers' Conference Special, en route from Euston to Preston in September 1975, with D. H. Constable, Area Manager, Southern Area, Rhodesia Railways

as it were, with two miles at an inclination of 1 in 37, leaving his successors a bugbear in operation that lasted for 120 years. The locomotive men were in trouble from the word go. One can think of many severely graded sections of line that became troublesome as loads increased and there was need for higher speed, but there was no time lag on the Lickey. By the oddest of circumstances the first distant glimpse of a solution came from America. Captain Moorsom, engineer of the line and the man to whom posterity is indebted for the bugbear of the Incline, had been in the USA and seen some of the celebrated Norris 'rear-driver' locomotives at work. He came back full of enthusiasm and promptly ordered fourteen engines of the type, which were built in Philadelphia. But they were tiny little things, as can be appreciated from the model of one of them in the Science Museum, South Kensington.

It was a far cry from the year 1840, when the little Norris engines first started puffing up the Lickey Incline with five or six small wagons in tow, to conditions on the Midland Railway some eighty years later, when a northbound express would often have four engines —two in front and two in rear—to labour up the incline at about 15 m.p.h.; and it was to alleviate this situation that Derby took an extraordinary step. Midland locomotive policy from 1906 onwards had been to have swarms of small standard engines, and use two when loads were increased, on passenger and goods trains alike; but in 1920 a single enormous ten-coupled engine specially for banking trains up the Lickey was built. Nothing like it, before or since, had ever been produced at Derby. It was intended to do the work of two six-coupled tank engines. Whether or not the ultimate intention was to build more of these giants I do not know; but *Big Bertha*, as she was affectionately known at Bromsgrove, remained the only one of her kind, and by the year 1949 when I went there to see the operations she had become something of a legend.

Banking trains up the Lickey was an extraordinary duty. Even on a busy day you would be standing by for half an hour or so, buffer up behind a northbound train, and then flail the engine 'all out' for about eight minutes, if it were a passenger, or fifteen minutes with a goods. Then you coasted back down the incline and waited for the next job. *Big Bertha* could not do all the banking, and in the summer of 1949 there were six of the little 'Jinty' tank engines also constantly in steam, for a fortnight at a stretch. Each engine, 'Jinties' and *Big Bertha*, alike, was continuously manned, three crews to each in the twenty-four hours, and the only respite from hard slogging duty took place at the change of shift, when the first duty of the oncoming crew was to clean the fire. I joined the men on *Big Bertha*. Normally one expects locomotive enginemen, drivers particularly, to be men well past their youth, but the two cheery young stalwarts on this huge engine looked mere boys. While we waited for our first job, the first section of a Bristol–Newcastle express, the universal, world-wide comradeship of the footplate quickly brought us into animated conversation, and I learned that their combined ages did not add up to my own; and that was twenty-seven years ago!

Banking on the Lickey Incline required a wealth of slick movement, good judgment, and plenty of brawn. Our train arrived from the south with ten coaches on, hauled by a Midland compound, and the moment her tail was clear of the points we followed smartly out. The scheduled stop is just one minute, in which time the points had got to be set, and we buffered gently up behind—our young driver handling the big engine as if she was a minicar. Directly we were in contact he whistled; back came the acknowledging whistle from the front end, and we were off. Our tough young teenager on the shovel had built up an enormous fire; we had a full head of steam, and soon *Big Bertha* was going absolutely all out. It is very rare that one sees a steam locomotive worked thus, but this engine was designed to be hammered, and hammered she had to be to provide any worthwhile assistance to the train engine on this extraordinary incline. I have many times been thrilled on the footplate, and I made several more trips up the Lickey; but I shall always remember that first eight minutes on *Big Bertha*, not least for the zest and skill of the two young men that handled her. When we got up to Blackwell and the crest of the bank, the driver's 'flatout' technique changed once more to that delicacy of touch he had shown when we buffered up. We eased up, as the express drew away, and rode gently into the lay-by siding.

We could not return to Bromsgrove at once, because the line was needed for a southbound express freight train. While we waited, however, I was rewarded by another great sight. The second section of the Bristol–Newcastle express came up the bank. It was headed by one of the famous 'Black Five' 4–6–0s, and was heavy enough to need *three* 'Jinties' to assist in rear. None of the Lickey bank engines are coupled in any way, and as they came in sight round the long curve north of Blackwell station, it was indeed a spectacle. The exhausts from those three little engines were going straight up, sky-high, to a terrific cacophony of sound; and, as they passed, first the rearmost one shut off, and dropped behind, leaving the other two still going full blast. Then the second shut off, and finally the third. Very quickly the trio joined us on the middle road, and then all four engines were ready to go down to Bromsgrove for their next jobs.

The first time I saw the Travelling Post Office in action was at

Fig. 2 TPO traductor apparatus

Llandudno Junction, in 1921. The outward- and inward-bound day Irish Mails then passed through within a few minutes of each other, and both trains set down and picked up mails without stopping. There was a path at the lineside where I could watch the postmen fixing the bags to be collected on the standards and making any necessary adjustments to the receiving nets. On the London and North Western Railway in those days, too, there was a fascinating variety of locomotives on these big trains. Unfortunately the time of day was most inconvenient. I was still only a schoolboy, and pedal as hard as I might afterwards I was always late for lunch back in Llandudno itself, where the family were staying on holiday. My watching of the Irish Mails always incurred strong parental displeasure—for what I always felt were quite trivial domestic reasons! So I did not see these famous trains as often as I would have liked.

There was always a particular appeal for me about mail trains, especially those which carried Travelling Post Offices equipped with the traductor apparatus. This interest was captured by the famous model engineering firm of Bassett-Lowke, which with characteristic ingenuity produced a working model of a TPO van, in various popular sizes of that time, by which the model railway owner could pick up mails at speed on his layout; and I began to study the elaborate network of TPO services that extended over the railways of Britain. To appreciate why it was then so elaborate it must be recalled that in the early 1920s road transport was in its infancy, and a train like the early morning Midland TPO, coming south, would set down mails by the traductor apparatus at many wayside stations serving country districts, rather than discharge large quantities of bags at the bigger centres like Gloucester and Bristol, for distribution from there. It was not, however, until after the Second World War, and then in response to a literary commission, that I was able to see TPO working from the inside: to visit major sorting offices, to travel on the trains, in the vans and on the engines, and to see the complex and closely interwoven organization that then carried the mails of this country—almost entirely by night.

I had as my project a study of the Anglo–Scottish mails, and my attention became centred upon the 8.30 p.m. from Euston to Glasgow and Aberdeen, the 'Down Special' TPO. This was then the main artery of mail traffic from south to north and, in addition to being primarily a Scottish train, it carried a great deal of English business as well. At various points en route other TPO and secondary mail trains fed into it, from Penzance, Cardiff, Aberystwyth, Bangor, Lincoln, Peterborough and Leeds, and at the time I did my travelling the men working the mail bag exchange apparatus had a busy time in the first hour out of Euston. Double summer time was then in force, and at mid-summer my friend Ernest Wethersett was able to photograph the exchange act at Harrow, with the sun still shining at 8.45 p.m. But to experience the full, gripping intensity of the mail one had to be on Crewe station in the hour before midnight. Four TPO trains preceded the arrival of the 'Down Special' from Euston: the 11.20 p.m. from Cardiff; the 11.30 from Shrewsbury, itself bound for York; the 11.34 from Birmingham; and the 11.35 from Bangor. Soon the platforms became a whirling pattern of trucks bringing mountains of mail ready for the 'Special' itself. These feeder services were all express passenger trains, on which a TPO carriage was conveyed; but the 'Special' was a purely postal train. All these trains had their own postmarks, and stamp collectors like myself took pleasure in having letters with postmarks like 'Shrewsbury–York TPO'; 'Midland TPO Going North'; 'Caledonian TPO Day Up', and so on.

I watched eagerly. The 'Cardiff' had been in some little time; the 'Bangor' arrived, and then the 'Down Special' was signalled. Out in the darkness far down the line it was soon recognizable by the chain of brilliant lights carried low down on the sorting carriages; threading its way through a succession of crossover roads it drew slowly in, with the unusual load of fourteen vehicles. Everything was steam worked in those days, and the engine was a 'Royal Scot'. Post Office Headquarters at St Martins-le-Grand, London, had deputed a very charming inspector, C. E. Martin by name, to be with me on all my travels, and with his introduction I now entered the 'holy of holies', the sorting carriages of the 'Down Special'. At that time there were five of them, two for Aberdeen, and three for Glasgow, marshalled together towards the rear of the train. On that Bassett-Lowke model of mine as a youngster I had wondered why the gangway connections at each end were not in the middle, but set to one side; now it was obvious. All along the right-hand sides of the carriages, looking north, were the pigeonholes for letter sorting with a wide table below and, unless the end gangways were offset, the tables would be an obstruction to men passing from one carriage to another, carrying sealed bags to the vans with the traductor mailbag exchange apparatus, and on other duties. The men were working like beavers. They had just taken over from the London men, and had begun their night's work in the Crewe sorting office at 9.30 p.m. Hardly a word was spoken; hardly a glance towards the open doors, beyond which the station platforms were buzzing with activity. But there was scarcely an ordinary passenger in sight. At that hour Crewe was given over almost entirely to mails.

We left on time, at 11.58 p.m., and, with the train soon making 70 m.p.h., Martin took me forward to the Aberdeen stowage van where the apparatus men were getting ready for a big discharge of mail at Warrington. Specially reinforced bags were used, strapped up in heavy black pouches. As I watched these being made ready my thoughts went back twelve years earlier to that early morning incident at Ballinluig, described in Chapter 5, when the unfortunate driver of the Highland Mail was 'clobbered' over the head by the pouch hanging on the lineside standard. On the 'Down Special' six pouches were to be put out at Warrington, and preparations were being made to use the traductors on the leading Aberdeen sorting carriage as well as the four in the stowage van.

Speed was high again on the short descent from Weaver Junction, and we passed over Moore water troughs at 69 m.p.h. A bar, painted red, was put across the gangway leading from the next carriage; from Moore Station we counted five overbridges, and then, swiftly, with one man at each door, the four bags in our van were fixed to the traductor arms. We swung over Acton Grange Junction; then came a hollow reverberation as we crossed the Ship Canal bridge; it was repeated at a second viaduct, over the Cheshire Old Cut. The apparatus men stood ready. One more landmark, the Mersey bridge; once we were over this the traductors were lowered, and the moving of a big lever extended the net. For me this turned out to be a very gentle introduction to the art of mail bag exchanging, as the train was being slowed down by adverse signals. But even though the speed was no more than 40 m.p.h., and only one pouch was collected, it came in with a hearty thud that shook the carriage.

From Preston onwards on this particular night I wore my other hat, or rather my overalls, for I had an engine pass. In 1948 the 'Down Special' was the fastest train over the line north of Crewe, being allowed only 101 minutes for the 90 miles from Preston to Carlisle, through the Westmorland Fells. The fastest passenger train then had 107 minutes, and in riding the *Queen Maud*, one of the fine 'Pacific' engines of the 'Princess Royal' class, my interest was switched temporarily from postal work to mechanical engineering.

The saga of the 'Down Special' from the TPO viewpoint was continued when some days later I joined the train in Carlisle station. Around 2 a.m. the big Citadel station seemed completely deserted; but the arrival of the 7.30 p.m. Perth express from Euston, at 2.13 a.m., brought the platforms to a state of great animation, and its departure still left many sleepy people about, including service men who had acquired the knack of sleeping soundly in apparently the most uncomfortable places and attitudes.

But soon one noticed, first in ones and twos, and then in larger groups, men who were very much alive at this hour in the morning, the sorters for the Caledonian and Edinburgh sections of the 'Down Special'; mail was piled high on the platforms, and the postal men glanced occasionally towards the platform intermediate signals. By this time the calling-on arm was pulled off, and a few minutes later in came the train, unannounced by the loudspeakers, to the mystification of many travellers. More than once I have seen gentlemen still in the mood for prolonging a convivial evening, fiercely remonstrating with the postal staff when their entrance to the train was barred!

Our engine this time was an un-rebuilt 'Royal Scot', and although I was too absorbed by the postal work to take any detailed timings, I could tell that our running was not so lively as on the night when I rode on the *Queen Maud*, and nearing Beattock we were slowing down to take banking assistance to the summit. The postal nets are on the north side of Beattock station, and with the train stopping there was ample opportunity to study in slow motion the working of the traductor arms. This particular journey was made in midsummer and it was now broad daylight. The arms were spring-loaded and remained in a vertical position close against the carriage side; when the mail pouches were pushed out their weight overcame the tension of the springs and the arm was pulled down into a horizontal position. To prevent the bags swaying unduly the traductor arm was steadied by means of a cord, as the pouches were swung into position for dispatch.

The train engine and the 'banker' exchanged greetings on their whistles and we started away. Directly we were through the first overbridge the pouches were lowered, and at this slow speed I was able to lean right out and watch the operation. There was a sharp click as the two pouches went, a clang as the traductor arms shot back automatically to the vertical, a cheery wave from the postman at the lineside, and we were away up the bank.

At Carstairs the Aberdeen and Glasgow sections were separated, the former leaving first after a stop of only five minutes. There was just time for me to climb down and see that our fresh engine, to take us on to Perth, was a Midland compound. I had a special interest in her, for I was bound for the footplate again from Stirling northwards; but the intervening stretch promised to be one of the busiest I had ever seen at the 'apparatus', and, fortified by a rich brew of 'TPO Special', that brand of tea reputedly so strong that in it a spoon will stand upright, we set off for the north.

We swept down Cumbernauld Glen, speed well over 60 m.p.h. In the vans a heavy dispatch was being prepared. At Carmuirs West the mail for Falkirk is set down, followed immediately afterwards by that for Larbert. At Carmuirs the postal net is just opposite the signal box, and the Larbert one is less than a mile farther on between Larbert Junction and the station. We came down the bank from Greenhill at nearly 70 m.p.h., with six pouches for Carmuirs ready fixed to the traductors; the two Larbert pouches were on the van floor ready to be fixed the moment the Carmuirs ones had gone. At this speed there was only a matter of seconds in which to do the job. The short tunnel after Camelon Junction provided the first recognition mark; just after this the Carmuirs pouches were lowered, and at 62 m.p.h. they were caught in the net. With lightning fingers the Larbert bags were made fast on the arms, and the operator then had comfortable time to look out and note precisely his mark for lowering the Larbert dispatch.

The sun was up on a gloriously fine morning when we got to Stirling but, on going up to the engine and presenting my credentials, I was momentarily taken aback when the cheery old Scots driver said: 'Och, if ye're on he-er ye're the dr-r-river'! Fortunately I knew the technique of handling a Midland compound, and knew the road reasonably well, with Jaimie Neill at my elbow. But, as everywhere else with the 'Down Special', one has to *run.* In the three-part article that I wrote afterwards there was a detailed log of that trip from Stirling to Perth; but only now, after nearly thirty years, can

I reveal in all due modesty that I was the driver. We were stopped by signal at Bridge of Allan, right on the heavy gradient of the Dunblane Bank; but even under my inexpert touch that willing engine lifted her train away and, with some nice free running after Gleneagles, up to 75 m.p.h., we covered the remaining 30 miles to Perth in 33¾ minutes. I handed the engine back to Neill for the final run in, for the track layout is complicated and I would not have known where along the lengthy platform we were required to stop. By the time I climbed down from that engine I had forgotten all about mails!

# 7 Days and Nights in Yards

On the face of it there might not seem to be anything very exciting or romantic in shunting railway trucks. The only relief, if one might call it so, from this most tedious of operations lay in the hazards and outright danger faced sometimes by the shunters riding on the moving wagons, or running beside them to apply the hand brakes. In the bigger yards shunting was a round-the-clock job, to be carried on regardless, even in the worst extremes of weather. It could equally be regarded as a slow and hopelessly inefficient process, quite apart from the damage often caused to consignments by the occasional rough-shunt or derailment of an individual wagon. Before the nineteenth century was out the more progressive of operating men were devising means of streamlining the whole process of freight train marshalling, and the steps that were taken were gradual; indeed, throughout the present century the methods leading to mechanization and automation have been in a continuous process of evolution, to such an extent that even today it cannot be said that finality has been attained. My own association with the design of apparatus for marshalling yards began more than forty years ago, and continued at intervals throughout my professional career.

To describe some of the adventures my friends and I had 'out the line' in testing and commissioning the equipment of today would, however, be rather like 'playing Hamlet without the Prince of Denmark', because we came in when the great principles of modern yard operation had been established, and it was a case of designing apparatus to meet the ever-increasing demands of the operators. So, a brief word is needed about the transition from the tedium, slowness and inefficiency of 'flat' yards, in which every movement back and forth needed the power of a locomotive, to the gravity-assisted 'hump' yard, with its sidings laid out on the 'balloon' principle. It is of course taken as read that a big yard is needed in some place where lengthy freight trains arrive with wagon loads for many different destinations. Sorting has to be carried out and the wagons placed in sidings appropriate to the continuation of their journeys. The first yard with which I was associated was Whitemoor, near March in

Cambridgeshire, where lengthy coal trains from South Yorkshire were split up into loads for many different destinations in East Anglia.

The first step from the primitive was to create an artificial gradient so as to utilize gravity to minimize the use of locomotive power. Then the reception sidings were laid out so that a train could be sorted in one continuous movement, instead of by a lot of backward and forward shunting. With a locomotive in rear a train would be propelled to the crest of the gradient; a shunter would uncouple wagons, singly or to run in groups according to destination, while other men would be stationed in the yard to set the points so that successive 'cuts' were switched into the correct siding. It was still a fairly slow process, albeit a more streamlined one, because the speed of propelling was very slow and often halting, to give sufficient time between successive cuts for the men in the yard to operate the points. Time had to be allowed for wagons descending the gradient to draw away from their successors and sometimes this meant stopping the propelling movement, if no more than briefly.

The introduction of electric or pneumatic power for operating railway points, which was being successfully applied at large passenger stations in the early 1900s, opened the way to a great improvement in yard operation; but while this gave faster movement of switches and made possible a centralized control, the labour force in the yards was still high, and the shunters were still involved in dangerous work, running beside the wagons and applying the hand brakes. Once a wagon had rolled away from the crest of the gradient, or 'hump', there was no other way of checking its speed. If it was going too fast it would come up with a shattering crash against the wagons already in that siding; if it was a bad runner it could stop short, by a hundred yards or so, and involve the nuisance of getting a locomotive to push it down, after all other shunting was completed. I have seen a wagon have three out of its four axle bearings destroyed in a really rough shunt, to say nothing of what probably happened to the goods inside!

At the end of the First World War British railwaymen became intensely interested in an important American development, a rail brake or 'car retarder', by which a braking effect could be applied to individual wagons as they ran under gravity from the hump. These retarders consisted of long articulated beams on each side of the running rails, which could be made to close in and grip the wheels of a wagon as it passed through. Their outstanding value lay in their ability to compensate for the difference between good and bad runners, and between wagons routed into empty sidings and those that were nearly full. The speed of propelling was high enough to allow for the bad runners, with very little, if any, braking in the retarders, while a free runner would be appropriately checked. The American name 'tower' for what we call a signal box had a new significance in marshalling yards, because the control cabins were built very tall, so as to give the man operating the retarders the widest possible outlook over the yard. 'Control tower', indeed, became standard British terminology for such buildings.

It was at this stage in the development, at the end of the 1920s, that my own connection with it began. Westinghouse had strong American connections, and we studied the electro-pneumatic retarder of the Union Switch and Signal Company in much detail; but when the time came for the London and North Eastern Railway to equip the first of the two Whitemoor yards the Germans got in first. While the electric point operation was a signal engineer's responsibility, the brakes were decided upon by the Chief Mechanical Engineer, and the famous engine designer Sir Nigel Gresley, as he later became, felt that the German design was much simpler and more desirable than the Anglo-American, because ours had so many more pin joints. We equipped the second Whitemoor yard, but it was by way of being a preliminary skirmish as far as I was concerned, albeit involving a great deal of design work on apparatus that was soon to become obsolescent. My real involvement began in the 1950s, and then it was in two different, though closely related, directions.

The first of these concerned the retarders. Our American associates had, in the intervening twenty years, developed a much simpler form of electro-pneumatic actuation, and we had succeeded in getting this accepted for a big new yard to be commissioned at Temple Mills, near Stratford, East London. But when the British Railways Modernization Plan was launched in 1955, and many more yards were projected, it became evident that the competition for business would be intense, and costs would be critical. The new Anglo-American design of retarder had cast steel beams, about 20 ft long, of a special alloy. They had been very skilfully designed in the USA, with the main member, reinforcing ribs and attachments so disposed and of such cross-sections as to absorb the heavy multiple stresses that were set up when a wagon was running through the retarder and the braking force was applied. A casting was the ideal form of construction, because it could be designed like a bridge, with the greatest depth of beam at the centre, and the least at the two end supports. But as the demand for a greatly increased number of these beams loomed up, to meet the British Railways programme, the one British manufacturer who was prepared to cast these beams to our stringent specification was caught in a mild boom in the steel trade, could offer no more than long and protracted deliveries, and intimated also that the price would have to be increased. To have succumbed to these circumstances would have put us out of the retarder market. The director responsible told me bluntly that to obtain a fair share of the business the manufacturing cost of a retarder needed reducing to *half* its current figure, quite apart from the increase in price that the steel founders were threatening.

The only practical alternative to casting was rolling, to produce a uniform cross section like a rail, and preliminary calculations showed that we should need a section nearly three times as heavy as the heaviest rail that had ever been rolled in this country, and more than twice as heavy as the largest American rail. Who on earth would undertake such a job for us? At first nobody seemed to want to know. With one steel executive on Tees-side the only time I could get an appointment was by inviting him out to dinner, and the young engineer who accompanied me, and who had to do most of the slide-rule pushing, entered upon the evening's work with very cold feet! I tried Scotland, Yorkshire, and then—thank goodness!—West Cumberland. The Workington Iron and Steel Company were interested, and enthusiastic. As one of the largest manufacturers of steel rails they felt that on any job for rolling in connection with railways they ought to be in on it. It was then April 1958, and a long haul was ahead of us. Enthusiasm certainly carried us along, but we needed every bit of it, for the snags we met were legion. As first schemed out, the beam we wanted was too big to go into the Workington rolls. We had to alter the shape considerably, and at each of the many changes in design an exhaustive stress analysis had to be made. At that stage of course such analyses were purely theoretical. We kept our fingers tightly crossed, and hoped we had thought of everything! Then at last we were satisfied, and Workington were satisfied they could handle it.

We had a contract to install retarders at a new marshalling yard at Perth. These were of the American type, but Scottish Region of British Railways agreed that one of the four required on the job should be of the new type. It was a most important concession, because it would enable us to carry out exhaustive tests before the yard was brought into service. Then one cold and wet night in November I took the sleeper to Whitehaven. Next morning the first of our new beams was to be rolled at Workington, and understandably it was made something of an occasion. As finally designed it had worked out at three times the weight of their heaviest rail so far, and everyone was agog to see the first one produced. The rail mill was open at one end; the wind was high and the rain drove in. I shall never forget the sight of that section, which by that time was verily engraved on my mind, coming almost white hot from the rolls. We built many retarders after that, and I have seen them handling heavy freight marshalling in many parts of the world—in Australia, in India, in New Zealand, as well as in many yards in this country; but, gratifying though it has been to see a design that gave us so many heartaches in such widespread use, none of these visits surpassed the thrill of seeing the first beam come white hot through the rolls at Workington.

There was another side to that yard at Perth that had its lighter moments. The control of the retarders, and of the electro-pneumatic point operation, was to be centred on a console high up on the tower, and between us we decided that it would be good to have an operating panel with a curved format. The man in charge could then be positioned centrally, have a bird's-eye view over the yard, and have all the necessary push buttons, thumb switches and indication lights located radially, with himself at the centre. For several weeks, however, the senior draughtsman responsible for this part of the work was at the receiving end of a two-pronged assault: from the electrical boffins who wanted more and more sophisticated equipment introduced into the console, and from the production department of the works who had continuous cold feet about the circular format of the panel. Then there was an occasion when I had been in London all day, and was late back home. I found the following scribbled on the telephone message pad: 'Westinghouse rang up; couldn't understand much, but it was something to do with a birth control panel'! This hilarious story quickly reached board level in our company. I was told it became a firm favourite with our Chairman who was something of a *raconteur*, and told over drinks in not a few London clubs. It certainly passed the test of a really good story—one that the club bore tells back to you a fortnight later.

Club stories or not, the Perth semicircular type of control panel became a standard product, and we eventually built quite a number of them. The works made a fine job of the metalwork, forming the curved sections with skill, but we were then on the threshold of a new development, making these artistically styled consoles in glass fibre. I must not, however, dilate on what were purely production problems. As time went on additional requirements arose in the operation of the retarders, and a contract for a yard on the Swedish State Railways, near Stockholm, gave us some problems. We had been very fortunate in the co-operation we had enjoyed from British Railways in having almost unlimited facilities for testing and experimenting on that first rolled-beam retarder installed at Perth. It was equally necessary to do some proving trials on the new controls embodied in the Swedish models, but we could hardly go to British Railways, and ask for space and wagons to try out the new design. There was nothing for it but to do the work on our premises at Chippenham.

There was a piece of open ground beside my colliery equipment test track, with sufficient length to build an inclined ramp on which the running of wagons in a marshalling yard could be simulated; but we needed rails, to make up about 200 yards of line. I have no doubt that my friends up at Workington would have been delighted to sell us some, at a price, to which would have to have been added transport charges over practically the length of England for about 20 tons of steel. But we did not need new rails for this ramp, and knowing the way main-line rails are gradually downgraded, as they get worn, first to branch lines, and then to sidings, I rang up Hector Lakeman, then Divisional Engineer of Western Region, at Bristol. He laughed: 'You could not have come at a better moment. We're re-laying in Box Tunnel,'—only 5 miles from Chippenham—'You can have some of those.' They were duly delivered 'over the fence' as it were, because the place we were going to build the ramp abutted on the top of the railway embankment just to the east of Chippenham station.

My test engineer and his men enjoyed their spell of 'railway' construction. The only slight hazard was that the ramp led downhill towards the railway, and if by any chance the operation of the retarder at the foot of the ramp was misjudged, or something went wrong, a wagon could go careering off the end of our track, through the boundary fence, and down the cutting side on to the 'real' railway! So we turned the ends of the rails upwards in a steep incline to check a possible runaway. For our tests we only needed one wagon, which could be loaded as required, and we selected one that was due to be scrapped from the 'condemned' yard at Swindon. A winch was installed whereby we could haul this wagon up to the top of the ramp, and then—hey presto!—we were in business.

The ramp was finished ready for a short section of retarder with the new mechanism to be installed and tried. It worked well, and we awaited the visit of the Swedish engineers. Five of them came over, a charming group, as pleasant to deal with in their erudition, as in their quiet courtesy and wide-ranging interests. They loved our ramp. They climbed all over it, called for innumerable tests, which our men gave gladly, even when requested repeatedly, because of their innate friendliness. The time came for them to return to Stockholm. We were given the 'right away' for bulk production, and I arranged a little farewell dinner party. It was high summer. They came to 'Silver Cedars' for drinks, a walk round our garden and a quick look at my model railway. It was a convivial occasion, and we were in no hurry to proceed to our chosen restaurant for dinner.

Then, in one of the few lulls in the conversation, one of them said quietly 'Is it the whisky, or do I hear birds?'

On British Railways, where all this manifold activity began with the launching of the Modernization Plan, it is ironic to reflect that the marshalling yard is now rapidly becoming obsolete. The modern philosophy of freight traffic operation is to run what are termed 'block loads': set formations of wagons that are not changed. There are the 'merry-go-round' coal trains shuttling back and forth between the collieries and the power stations, loading and discharging their cargo in single streamlined operations; there are the company trains chartered and run to regular schedules, carrying cement in bulk, oil and motor car bodies. There are the liner trains, consisting of a fixed rake of flat bogie wagons, on to which containers are loaded. These need no marshalling, and some of the older yards—including Perth—are now closed. But what has become obsolescent on the increasingly streamlined British Railways is still being developed overseas, and I shall never forget the hours I spent watching operations from the tower in the gigantic yard of the Canadian Pacific at Calgary. There, true enough, were all the manifold disciplines in electrical control that we had applied at Perth, Carlisle, Middlesbrough and elsewhere, but the master control was by computer. I admired the precision of the working and the accuracy of the end product; but how the result is achieved, I am afraid, passes the comprehension of my three score years and ten!

# 8 Travels in Continental Europe

From a very early stage in my railway reading I was fascinated by the Lötschberg line, though it was not until the late spring of 1967 that I was able to study it on the spot. It is the most recently completed of the great Alpine railways of Switzerland and, as far as main line mileage is concerned, much the smallest; but, in the stupendous grandeur of its scenery, its superb engineering and impeccable traffic operation, it can be regarded as one of the whole world's finest. Except through the great Lötschberg Tunnel, which in many ways is the centrepiece of the line, the track is single throughout, and some years ago when I was engaged in editing a handbook on single line railways I had written to the management of the Bern-Lötschberg-Simplon, to give it its full name, asking a number of questions about their operation. In a prompt and charming reply they suggested that as one of their officers, M. Jean Perret, would be in London in the near future, I should meet him for a talk. A week or so later he arrived in the lounge of the Great Western Royal Hotel at Paddington, carrying an obviously very heavy suitcase, and after identifying each other, we got to work.

Like all Swiss of executive status he spoke English fluently, and with much penetrating comment handed over timetable diagrams, gradient profiles, brochures covering locomotive history and very much more. Noting that I had no more than a small brief case, and that I seemed a little embarrassed by the sheer weight of literature that he was unloading on me, he laughed and said drily 'Heavy documentation!' At that moment however the waiter brought our tea, and our friendship, which was rapidly warming, turned to more general topics. By this time I had sensed a slight French inflexion in his speech, and was not surprised to learn that his family came from Geneva. The railway itself runs through territory that is almost entirely German speaking; but more of that later. On that first meeting such was the volume of literature he unloaded on to me that eventually I had to ask the hall porter of the hotel to rustle up some brown paper and string to make a secure parcel.

About three years later when my wife and I were planning a

holiday in Switzerland that was to include nearly a week at Interlaken, I wrote to the BLS again asking if they would permit me to ride in the cabs of their electric locomotives over the mountain section between Spiez, on Lake Thun, and Brig. To my great pleasure they replied that M. Perret would come with me, and also suggested that my wife should travel in the trains 'to enjoy the ride'. All the modern Swiss carriages have what the Americans call 'picture windows', and from them the passing scene can be enthralling; but to ride in the cab of an electric locomotive, heading into the highest regions of the Bernese Oberland, is an incomparable experience. I write this with full recollection of later journeys, on spectacular routes in Australia and India, and having ridden through the Canadian Rockies in the cab. On the BLS there was much to see besides scenery. No traveller on the Continent will have failed to note at some time how stationmasters are out on the platform to see every train go through, whether it is stopping or not, and 5 miles out from Spiez, on passing Reichenbach, I saw one of those artistic touches that contribute to the precision of Swiss railway operation. On this first trip we did not have a very heavy load and were getting slightly ahead of time. The stationmaster gave the recognized hand signal that we should slow down a little. Otherwise we should not have made our crossings with trains coming in the opposite direction at exactly the right times and would have to stop accordingly. In the course of our 45¾ mile journey from Spiez to Brig we had to cross four northbound trains at intermediate passing loops, and a fifth train on the double-line section through the Lötschberg Tunnel.

The heaviest part of the climb up to the tunnel begins at Frutigen, where the gradient becomes 1 in 37. But gradients do not worry the electric locomotives of the BLS. The whole timetable of the line is based on a uniform speed of 47 m.p.h. uphill and downhill alike. Higher speed downhill is not possible because of the constant and severe curvature. And now, as we made our way uphill from Frutigen, we were climbing into an arena of mountain peaks of breathtaking splendour; yet even a gradient as steep as 1 in 37 could not get us up to the *cul-de-sac* of Kandersteg in the distance that lay between. Where there is such a dramatic terrain Swiss engineers had been the first to devise the ingenious procedure of constructing spirals, often entirely tunnelled into the mountainsides, to gain height in the short horizontal distance between one valley level and another. They involved marvellous precision in surveying, seeing that they were on fairly severe curves and steep gradients, and often entirely in tunnel. So, from Frutigen we were soon traversing the spectacular spirals of Blausee, where one can see the line at three different levels on the same precipitous mountainside. Between each

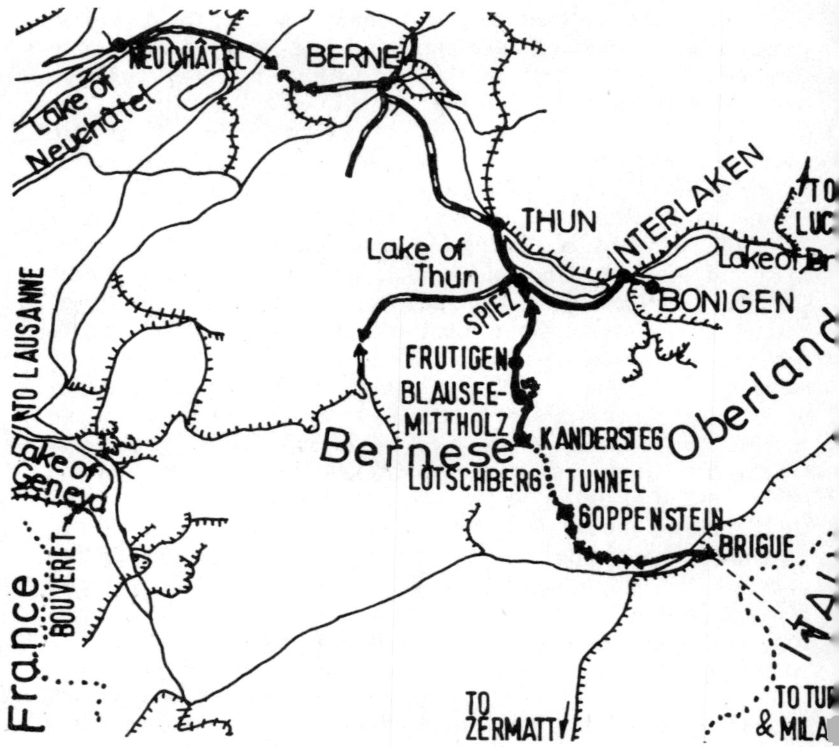


Fig. 3 The Bern–Lötschberg–Simplon Railway

successive level the line makes a complete spiral loop to gain height all the time on the continuous rising gradient of 1 in 37. We stopped briefly at Kandersteg, and there ahead of us was the great Lötschberg Tunnel, 9 miles long. Although it takes the railway at its centre point to an altitude of 4,025 ft above sea level it is, even there, several thousands of feet below the great mountains that tower overhead. In mid-tunnel we passed another train and, as the two approached each other, on their own tracks, headlights were dipped—a pleasing little act of courtesy.

Having left what might be called the picture postcard beauty of Swiss Alpine valley scenery at Kandersteg, we emerged at the south end, at Goppenstein, in the wild, forbidding and treeless Lonza

Gorge, and made our way downhill at 47 m.p.h. on a dizzy slope where the line is protected at frequent intervals by avalanche shelters. While we were thus running Jean Perret told me a good story of some technical visitors. They had come in the summer and been duly impressed by the mountains and the engineering works, and then they asked for how long was the line closed down in the winter! After momentary amazement at anyone having the idea that they closed at all, the BLS explained that the winter months were about their busiest times, with seasonal tourist traffic added to all their normal business. 'What about the snow?' came the next query, and the BLS people just laughed that one off with 'There's no time for it to settle. We've too many trains running.' This might seem a too facile reply, but actually there is a good example of this in the north of England, in the Settle and Carlisle and the Shap routes through the northern fells. On the former there have always been some long intervals between trains, and in severe weather they have had, over the years, some terrific snowblocks. The line over Shap runs through country that is just as bleak and exposed, but is much more heavily used, and it has never been so vulnerable to wintry conditions—indeed, I cannot recall a time when it has been blocked to any extent.

Returning to the Lötschberg, its last miles are a scenic delight. A long tunnel takes the line from the desolation of the Lonza Gorge to a shelf on the mountainside overlooking the Rhone valley, and on curves continuously following the contour of the hills we ride gently downhill to our junction with the Jura–Simplon main line of the Swiss Federal Railways, at Brig. The train was going forward through the Simplon Tunnel into Italy, but on this occasion Brig was the turning point for us. I have said that Jean Perret was a versatile linguist. On the run from Spiez he had been talking as fluently to our German-speaking driver as he conversed with me in perfect English; and of course his native tongue was French. But wait! He took my wife and me into the pleasant little town and sought a restaurant for lunch. He chose a delightful little old-world hostelry, not the kind of place the ordinary tourist would patronize, but something peculiarly and exclusively Swiss. Alas, when the buxom young waitress came to attend to us, she spoke in a dialect that he could not understand at all. Neither could she understand his German, or his French, which he tried in desperation. It took two more members of the staff, summoned from the inner recesses of the establishment, plus a little pigeon English, to sort out our needs. Before we had finished the six of us had become quite hilarious. It was a good start to an excellent lunch.

The Lötschberg line was not completed until 1913, and I must next tell of travels over the oldest of all railways to penetrate the chain of the Alps, in this case at their eastern end. In the 1840s Austria was the premier power in Central Europe, if not in the entire Continent. The German Empire was yet to come, and the city of Vienna was a focus of trade and culture. The general flow of traffic of all kinds was from north to south, from the Baltic to the Adriatic. The first railway in Austria had been built in 1837, northwards from Vienna, and it is not surprising that thoughts soon turned to the possibilities of a route to the south, aimed towards the great port of Trieste. The building of the great line over the Semmering Pass is one of the great epics of early railway history; but here I can only tell of how I saw it more than a hundred years later from the cab of the electric locomotive working The Austria Express, a celebrated international train that continued through Yugoslavia and Greece to complete a journey of no less than 1,300 miles by the time its through carriages reached Athens. Once again, from that unrivalled viewpoint, I was able to appreciate something of the way the first projectors of the railway were overawed by nature when it came to finding a way through these easternmost ranges of the Alps. Here were no gigantic summits like those of the Bernese Oberland, nor a tremendous continuous range, like that of the Canadian Rockies or the Andes; it was just a wild, confused tumult of high rocky eminences, densely wooded, in which anyone projecting a railway would have had the greatest difficulty in getting anything of a distant view on which to focus his sights.

As we mounted the steep gradient I watched, entranced. I had two cameras at the ready on the flat-topped dashboard of the locomotive, and at the speed we were going, 35 to 40 m.p.h., I paused frequently in my technical note-taking to photograph some gem of scenery, or some item of interest on the line. The higher we mounted, looking down upon the tumbled wilderness of limestone crags, the more rapid became succession of tunnels and viaducts. The line is double-tracked throughout, and the engineering is magnificent. The greatest spectacle of all is the Kalte Rinne Viaduct. Even seen from the footplate the geography of the Semmering Mountains can be most confusing, with viaduct following tunnel, deep ravines on one side, towering crags on the other. Then after a dramatically picturesque section there comes a tremendous swing round to the left, and crossing this deep valley is the Kalte Rinne Viaduct. It has the two-arch form of construction, with a second row of arches beneath the upper set, and such is the alignment of the track that I was able to photograph the viaduct broadside on from the left-hand cab window of the locomotive a few minutes after we had crossed it in the opposite direction. Soon after we reached the summit of the line, at Semmering station, 2,900 ft above sea level and 65 miles from

Vienna. It was our first stop, and the run had taken 82 minutes.

I was travelling with Dr Adolf Giesl-Gieslingen, inventor of the Giesl oblong ejector, one of the last appliances introduced to improve the efficiency of steam locomotives, and widely used in his native Austria. It came, unfortunately, too late in the history of the steam locomotive to stem the onrush of the diesel in Great Britain and many other countries; but the principles so ingeniously applied had a remarkable effect on steam production, as I shall tell later from some experiences in Kenya. The main line we were following continues down the beautiful Mur Valley into Styria, and at Bruck it bifurcates. The electrified line continues south-west towards the Italian frontier, but our train was to follow the Mur Valley further to Graz, and eventually to the Yugoslav frontier. This latter route is not electrified, and Dr Giesl had not been sure whether we should be steam or diesel hauled after Bruck. Our authority gave permission to ride on either. We had both brought overalls and 'sweat rags' in readiness, and when we arrived at Bruck we were both delighted to see a big Austrian 4–6–4 steam tank engine waiting to take us forward. We climbed into our 'party clothes' on the station platform, and were ready to board the fresh engine when it backed down, appropriately equipped with one of Dr Giesl's ejectors. Although the driver and fireman had not a word of English between them, a footplate pass and a pair of dirty overalls immediately established that innate friendship of the footplate that transcends any barrier of language, creed or colour; and on learning who their second 'passenger' was these cheery enginemen were delighted beyond measure.

At this stage I must tell a story about Dr Giesl's elder daughter, a young lady of many parts who, at the same time, was an expert engineering draughtswoman, sang in the chorus of the Vienna State Opera, and was a tough 'outdoor' girl, on one visit of ours preferring walking down from the summit of the Schneeberg to riding in the mountain train, and reaching the base station at Puchberg before us. Well, one day she was out walking on the left bank of the Danube, and missed the last passenger train back into Vienna. She was at a small country station wondering what to do when a local goods train rolled in, hauled by one of the smaller and older tank engines. But Willi saw at once that it was fitted with the Giesl oblong ejector, and immediately asked the driver for a lift to Vienna. He naturally refused, and the following is a free translation of the short argument that followed: 'My father designed the chimney of your engine.'—'How can you say that?'—'and I made the drawings.' She got her footplate ride.

Down at Bruck that day her father and I climbed into the cab of that tall '78' class 4–6–4. Tank engines in Austria, or anywhere else, are not famed for the roominess of their cabs, but once inside we were comfortably ensconced, out of the way of driver and fireman. Externally that engine was no showpiece. She was painted plain black and very much travel stained; but once under way she glided along like a veritable Rolls-Royce. By that time in my steam footplate experience I had ridden all sorts and conditions of engines, from lumbering cart horses that could nevertheless run like stags, through sweet-riding thoroughbreds, to wild yawing things that scared the daylights out of me; but never do I remember one that ran so smoothly and silently as this Austrian 4–6–4 tank. Dr Giesl noted with pleasure also that the exhaust from her chimney was absolutely clear, showing that his oblong ejector was promoting the perfect combustion of the coal that it was designed to do. Some years later I had a striking exposition of this in a land far from Austria. I was 'out the line' in Japan with my friend H. Uematsu, watching the coal train workings in the northern island of Hokkaido, on a line where all trains were steam-hauled and mostly by the very numerous 'D 51' class of 2–8–2s. Japanese coal makes a lot of smoke, and on a bracing cold day in early spring these engines were providing magnificent exhaust effects for our cameras. Then a train approached, pounding hard up the gradient, but showing an absolutely clear exhaust—most disappointing to photographers. Its engine was fitted with a Giesl ejector!

With the Austria Express we were running through scenery of very great charm. The winding valley of the Mur reminded me irresistibly of Symond's Yat in Monmouthshire, with the same steep, densely wooded slopes. The hills on either side were much higher, it is true; but the river softly flowing between level meads heightened the similarity, so much so that one would not have been surprised to round one curve in the line and see the stately ruin of Tintern Abbey ahead. The fruit trees were white with blossom and the meadows silvery with a profusion of clock-dandies. But instead of coming to some Styrian equivalent of Tintern we approached the dramatically perched castle of Judendorf, which was reminiscent of the Rhine rather than the Wye. To see this beautiful country amid the smells and incidental joys of a steam locomotive footplate merely added to the pleasure. But soon the deep valley was opening out. The town of Graz lay ahead, and this marked the end of our journey on that day.

Olivia and I returned from one of our holidays in the south by the Rheingold Express. It was then one of the fastest trains in Europe, and as far as I recall the only one then required to run regularly at 100 m.p.h. I was given permission to ride in the cab from Basel as far north as Karlsruhe, and it was a most impressive experience. It was not to be the first time I had ridden at 100 m.p.h. in the driver's cab, because I had been thrilled by a brief spell at 103 on a British steam locomotive some years earlier. But this was a regular run, surrounded by all the elaborate provisions that I have come to associate with modern German railroading. On the dashboard of the powerful electric locomotive was a book of oblong shape showing, to scale, a diagram of the line, the maximum speed permitted over each section, and a graph showing the speed that must be run in order to keep the schedule time of this train. As the journey progressed the pages of the book were turned over to correspond with each successive section of line. An official from headquarters met me at Basel Bad, bringing my engine pass; but he spoke no English, and German is not the language in which I am most fluent! Moreover, once in the cab this man started a rapid and animated conversation with the driver, which continued without a break, at the top of their voices, all the way to Karlsruhe. I have not the slightest idea what they were talking about!

Railway-wise I was particularly interested in the fast lap from Freiburg, for which 84½ miles only 58 minutes were allowed, start-to-stop. Because of some confusion and delay in marshalling up the train in Basel, we were running fourteen minutes late, and studying that book on the dashboard there did not seem to be much margin between the line maximum speed and the speed at which we had to run to keep our scheduled time. Between Basel Bad and Freiburg indeed the margin had not been enough to offset the effect of a slowing for track repairs, and we had taken 35¼ minutes, instead of the scheduled 34, to cover the 38½ miles of this initial start-to-stop run. These upper reaches of the Rhine valley pass through flat and uninteresting country, in striking contrast to the dramatic scenery below Wiesbaden; but the railway is not entirely straightforward from the high-speed running point of view. There were speed restrictions to 40 m.p.h. at Offenburg, 75 at both Achern and Bühl, and 60 m.p.h. at Bietigheim. Between these restrictions it was necessary to run at 100 m.p.h. the whole time. The locomotive rode very smoothly at this high speed, and in the flat, open country one soon lost any particular sensation of very fast travel. Again I noted the recovery margin was slight, for although we were running practically up to the line maximum all the way, we regained no more than a single minute of the time lost at Basel, even though our average speed was all but 89 m.p.h.

For once I was rather glad to leave the footplate. Concentration on collecting the technical data I needed amid the torrent of conversation in a foreign language had left me with a splitting headache;

but a quiet cup of tea with my wife and a sojourn in the dome car soon put things right, and I was ready to enjoy *from the train* the thrills of 75 m.p.h. running round the incessant curves beside the Rhine from Bingen down to Bonn. It so happened that dinner was served on this particular section. While there was a *maître d'hotel* hovering in the background, the actual service was performed by a bevy of very efficient waitresses who, unlike my erstwhile companions on the footplate, were all multilingual. On the lapels of their tunics they wore flags of the countries whose language they spoke. None spoke less than three, English, French and German, and the head girl added Dutch and Italian for good measure. The northern termini of the Rheingold are in Holland. One might have imagined that part of the training of those girls was to keep their feet, balancing a well loaded tray, when the train was swinging round the curves, in and out of tunnels, opposite to the Lorelei Rock, with more leisurely freight trains pounding along the tracks on the right bank of the river. Their service was immaculate.

Homeward bound on another occasion I had an engine pass for the Golden Arrow, steam hauled, non-stop from Paris to Boulogne Ville. It was one of those faultless performances that were characteristic of the French railways in the heyday of steam. I had a burly, genial inspector named Baudry as my guide and philosopher and, although he had no English, I am better at French than German and we got on well. Moreover that steam cab was a placid, much more serene place than that of the 'E 10' electric on the Rheingold, and the entire journey was most enjoyable. Although speeds had not then risen to their present levels the Golden Arrow—or *Flèche d'Or*, as I should call it in France—was no laggard, and our cruising speed on level track was all the time near to the then legal maximum of 120 kilometres per hour—74½ m.p.h.

We passed the last station before Boulogne, Pont-de-Briques, a distance of 154¾ miles, in 146¾ minutes, and then slowed into the Town station. A man with a red flag appeared and walked solemnly ahead of us as we steamed funereally across the cobbled stones of the quay to the Gare-Maritime. We stopped, and I took a cordial farewell of my friends on the footplate before going to the exit, where my wife was waiting with a porter and our luggage. We were going straight on to the steamer for Folkestone, and there was no time for me to change out of overalls. In due course we came to the Customs examination. I showed my passport. The man behind the desk looked at the photograph in it, and then at me. He looked again. Passport photographs are traditionally not the best likenesses, but I did not think this one of me was all that bad. This Frenchman however had yet another double check before he handed me back my passport, with a slowly spreading grin on his face. When I got on to the steamer and went to discard my overalls and tidy up, I saw the reason why! Coal from the Pas de Calais is not the least dusty in the world, and my face was the colour of lead. I was reminded of the Scots lassie at the reception desk of the St Enoch Hotel in Glasgow, when I went in straight from riding a 'Royal Scot' locomotive through from Leeds, who exclaimed 'Ye'll no' be wantin' a wash!'

# 9 A Vigilance of Inspectors

In searching round to find a collective noun to embrace the *genus inspectus* I paused at 'snoop', 'harassment', and 'invigilation'. But a 'snoop of inspectors' was no more complimentary or true than a harassment of them, however much those experiencing their activities may have nurtured sentiments even more antagonistic than these—at times anyway! In actual fact, however, no words of mine are good enough to praise a body of men whose experience, sheer horse-sense and unflagging devotion to duty—whether on the track, in signal boxes, on the footplate, or in the service of railway contractors—has been, and still of course is, a massive contribution to the remarkable safety of railway operation.

In the fifty years of my association with railways I have certainly met some who would qualify as 'characters', involved in moments grave, gay and hilarious. But at the start I am reminded of the words of a great civil engineer, John Miller, of the North Eastern Area of the London and North Eastern Railway in the 1930s, speaking particularly of the permanent way inspectors, and drawing a vivid analogy between their role and that of sergeant-majors in the regular army, as portrayed in one of Kipling's famous Barrack Room Ballads. The military counterpart was far from the music hall caricature, but was rather the friend and counsellor of men under him, who 'learns to make men like 'im so they learn to like their work.' However much may be surveyed, estimated and designed by the technically trained staff, the actual job of carrying out the work on site, working inevitably against the clock, in whatever hazards of weather the appointed weekend might bring, is the responsibility of the permanent way inspector—who for a single renewal or modernization may have a work force of several hundred men at once.

In my earlier days with Westinghouse we had a great old inspector in north-eastern England, Alf Mattison by name. He was boss of what we called the Leeds Gang, which was a relic of the days when one of the principal constituents of our company, McKenzie and Holland, had a standing contract for installation of signalling on the old North Eastern Railway. Alf was a dyed-in-the-wool Yorkshire 'tyke', friendliness itself, and would always greet you with an 'allo-oa-oo', with a long drawn out, singing inflexion. He was one of that sturdy breed of men who would always speak to their bosses with respect, but with no fear or favour, and one of the best stories told of him concerned the erection of two very tall masts carrying telegraph wires across the river Aire, at Selby.

The river is navigable for a long distance inland, and to give the necessary clearance for the passage of ships—sailing ships too!—the main-line crossing at Selby was, and still is, by a swing bridge. The telegraph wires had to be carried over the waterway at such a height as to clear the masts of the tallest ships. McKenzie and Holland received an order to supply new masts of increased height. These were in the form of latticed steel towers, like enormously elongated signal posts, rising to about 60 ft above river bank level, and Alf Mattison had the job of erecting these, as usual for such operations on a Sunday morning. They got to work soon after daybreak, and then the manager of the Leeds Office arrived on the scene, and began to 'muscle in' on the operation. Now that manager eventually became a very high officer, and ended up with a seat on the Board; but old Alf had no two minds about it. He watched sardonically for a few minutes and then said 'Ee, Mister Powell, have you had your breakfast?' 'No, not yet.' 'Well I suggest you go and have it, and I'll get on w' t' job: else you get on w' t'job, and I'll have my breakfast.'

I was at Leeds one Sunday when a truly horrible changeover was in progress. It was a cold blustering day in November, when the old mechanical signalling was being replaced by colour lights and electro-pneumatic points. That it rained continuously from about ten in the morning was one of the hazards of life, but the railway civil engineer had decided to demolish one of the old signal boxes on this very day, and soon the whole drenching atmosphere was impregnated with clouds of flying brick dust. It got everywhere and stuck! Tempers began to get short by early afternoon, and the work was not going as rapidly as desired. The railway signal inspector was getting impatient. He stormed into the ground floor of the new cabin. 'A've been round t'job,' he shouted, 'gettin' bloody men to spark.' One of our senior engineers asked quietly 'Have you succeeded?' 'Aye'—but at that moment old Alf came in through the door, drenched to the skin I should think, and looking all in. He had been on the job since nine the previous evening. 'Aye,' repeated the railway inspector, 'all except Alf Mattison. Nothing could make him spark; he's too bloody wet!'

The corps of locomotive running inspectors had a different role. They were the eyes and ears of the drawing office, ensuring that engines were driven and fired correctly, and reporting back if any feature of equipment, or the locomotive as a whole, was not functioning properly. At one time the liaison was much closer than it has subsequently become. Up to the time of the grouping of the railways in 1923, the Chief Mechanical Engineers of the various railways, or Locomotive Superintendents as they were then more generally styled, were responsible for everything to do with locomotives and their working—design, construction, maintenance, repair, and actual working in traffic; and on the larger railways, such as the London and North Western and the Great Western, the CME, taking into account all the drivers, firemen, and shed staff on his payroll, in addition to main and subsidiary workshops, had many thousands of men under him. By 1922 only two railways, the Midland and the South Eastern and Chatham, had broken away from this old tradition. The locomotive running inspectors had a roving commission of a rather specialized kind. Their authority over the drivers and firemen was largely of an advisory kind, and they had to investigate in cases of difficulty, either in handling individual engines, or in maintaining schedule time. They were mostly recruited from the senior express drivers, and thus knew the job from their boyhood upwards. Not all drivers welcomed their presence on the footplate. I remember an occasion when I was to ride a fast express, and the driver happened to be a rather militant type. He rounded on the inspector who was to ride with me, saying 'What have you come for?' To which the inspector replied 'To do my job—and see you do yours!' This incident was in my experience so exceptional, however, as to be unique. Generally the inspector was guide and philosopher to all on board.

The extent to which the running inspectors were in the confidence of headquarters was shown by an incident in the early months of 1904. Eastbound transatlantic liners had begun calling at Plymouth, setting down by tender both passengers and mails. By tacit agreement the London and South Western Railway took the passengers, while the Great Western took the mails, and with this prestige traffic the arrival of each liner was followed by an unofficial, and at first no more than mildly provocative, race to London, the goals being Waterloo and Paddington. But as time went on the rivalry intensified. The mighty Dugald Drummond was then Chief Mechanical Engineer of the LSWR and he began to put the pressure on his enginemen to step up the running, while on the Great Western G. J. Churchward, who only two years earlier had attained the chieftainship of the locomotive department, was equally determined not to be beaten. He selected one of the running inspectors at Newton Abbot, George Flewellyn by name, and gave him responsibility for all locomotive working on the Ocean Mails, as they became known. He was still in the saddle as Chief Locomotive Inspector of the GWR when I first began to travel, but I never met him personally. He had retired before I made my first footplate journeys. His grandson worked for Westinghouse, however, and had a fund of stories of the 'old man'.

One of the best concerns the period of build-up towards the 'Record of Records' made on 9 May 1904. Churchward was watching developments closely. His new 'City' class 4–4–0 engines were nearly always used on the Ocean Mails between Plymouth and Bristol, and he was eager for news of their technical prowess, as in the mounting heat of competition they were stage by stage stepping ahead of what Drummond's engines were doing on the LSWR. There was no doubt that the 'Cities' were proving among the fastest engines that had ever run the rails, in Britain or anywhere else; but Churchward was anxious not to reveal his full hand too soon. Flewellyn was summoned to Swindon, and after a characteristically forthright homily Churchward concluded: 'Withhold any attempt at a maximum speed till I give the word. Then you can go and break your bloody neck!' The outcome of this was the exploit by which the *City of Truro* is immortalized—a speed of 100 m.p.h. down the Wellington Bank, in Somerset, as mentioned again in Chapter 11.

If Flewellyn was the first to 'do the ton' on British railways, and, as far as fully authenticated records can be traced, first in the whole world, it was Sam Jenkins of the London and North Eastern Railway who holds a record that is likely to stand for all time—the maximum ever attained with a steam locomotive, 126 m.p.h. And Jenkins I came to know well. I met him first on some braking trials between King's Cross and Peterborough. Sir Nigel Gresley's famous streamlined trains had been introduced before the vacuum brake equipment was adequate for the stopping distances prescribed by the existing signalling system, and to ensure safety in operation the Silver Jubilee, the Coronation, and the West Riding Limited were all 'double-blocked' south of York; in other words two complete sections ahead had to be clear before the block signal could be lowered. Westinghouse were developing a 'quick-service application' valve which gave much reduced stopping distances from high speed, and on certain Sundays tests were being carried out jointly by Gresley's own staff and Westinghouse. Jenkins was the King's Cross locomotive inspector looking after things on the footplate.

It was not an easy assignment. Quite unlike the running of a service train, the tests required the precise attainment of certain speeds at definite locations on the line, and from these the making of test stops. Even on a Sunday there were other trains about, and after some of these prescribed stops we had to draw into loops to allow regular trains to have a clear run through. Furthermore the drivers varied from week to week, because the first top-link man available for an extra duty was put on to the job. Inevitably some were more adaptable than others to the special test requirements, and at times Jenkins found himself virtually driving the engines. The streamlined 'A 4' 'Pacifics' were fitted with Flaman speed recorders, which made a continuous graph of the speed throughout a run. These were used primarily to keep a check on driver's work, and to ensure as far as possible that the stipulated speed restrictions along the line were not exceeded. At the end of all the service runs the chart was taken from the recorder and sent in a sealed container to locomotive running headquarters for scrutiny.

On these brake trials the continuous record was not made, but the pointer of the speedometer was used to guide the drivers in regulating the speed. At the same time it was considered essential to have an exact measure of the speed at the moment of brake application, and this was made by various observers in the train, by stop watch from the mileposts. The senior Westinghouse brake engineer, Louis Le Clair, who despite his name was a Glaswegian Scot, loved to take a hand in this. Clad in a Balaclava helmet, goggles and a huge muffler, and looking for all the world like an Eskimo, he used to hang out of an open window, trying to spot the mileposts through smoke and steam. On occasions I took a hand in the stop-watching, and when steam was beating down and mileposts were hard to see I had difficulty in convincing them that clocking the wheel-beats over the rail joints was just as accurate as working off the mileposts. But it was all good clean fun, and there was a rare spirit of *camaraderie* between railway engineers and Westinghouse on these Sunday jaunts to Peterborough. Many of these trips were made in the depths of winter, and we were all ravenously hungry and simply fell on the buffet lunch that was laid on for us—none more heartily than the burly Jenkins himself.

One day when I was a member of the Westinghouse team there was a tearing east wind going. It happened to be an occasion when comparative figures were being collected for the old standard, rather than the improved vacuum, brake. To the consternation of the designer of the QSA valve, an incredible character by the name of Aloysius Brackenbury, we were getting better stops without his valve than any previously attained with it! But I could hear that the engine was having to be worked tremendously hard to get the speeds we required, and during the lunch break at Peterborough I questioned Jenkins as to how the engine was being driven. His reply was brief: 'We've just about murdered the old thing!' I told Le Clair. It was not the standard vacuum brake but the wind that was giving us such excellent stops that day, and by the time we got back to King's Cross we all agreed that the data we had collected was, to quote one of the more expletive of the Westinghouse staff, 'a lot of codswallop.' In the summer of 1954 the London–Edinburgh non-stop was accelerated to a six-and-a-half-hour run, making an average speed of just over 60 m.p.h., and with the train itself bearing the gracious title of The Elizabethan it was more than ever an absolutely show turn. Business had taken me to Scotland about the time the new service was inaugurated, and I was able to travel south on only the second day. Jenkins had come up on the footplate on the Monday and, when we met on Waverley station the following morning, he invited me to ride on the engine for part of the return trip. He was then an Eastern Region man, so his authority did not begin until the King's Cross men took over, at full speed, about ten miles north of York. A compartment in the train used to be reserved for the relief enginemen, and south of Darlington he came to where I was riding to say that they would soon be taking over, and that then I could come through when I liked. These engines were fitted with special tenders having a narrow corridor on the right hand side, and through this the relieving men passed at the appropriate time.

The Edinburgh men were finishing their part of the job in great style. We swept through Thirsk at 82 m.p.h., and soon afterwards Jenkins and the London driver and fireman prepared to go through. I went forward for a brief chat, to arrange that I would go through to join them after we passed Doncaster. Then all was consternation. The connecting door to the front gangway could not be opened! The lock worked, but the door was jammed. Jenkins was a big chap and he put his weight against it; no avail. The fireman dashed back to get the tools carried in case of accidents to free a trapped passenger; but all the time we were tearing towards York, covering each of the miles in about 45 seconds, and we could imagine the Scottish crew wondering where on earth the relief men were. They did not know the road south of York, and if the London men were not through by then they would have had to stop; and stopping the 'non-stop' was almost a hanging matter. The way that door was eventually forced, and the London men got through in time—just!—is an epic that would have needed a tape recorder to do full justice to the vocal accompaniments of the job!

This was no occasion for any speed records down the Stoke Bank. The engine was the *Golden Fleece*, and she was purring along with almost effortless ease. When I went through to the footplate at Doncaster we were $5\frac{1}{4}$ minutes early; but we needed that time in hand to cover a slowing on account of permanent way work near Newark. We went comfortably up the hill to Stoke Tunnel, and then the driver just let the engine make her own speed down towards Peterborough. We went up to a maximum of 96 m.p.h. and, when we were down to almost level grades, continued at 90 to 95 m.p.h. till we had to slow down for another permanent way check. To cut a long and fascinating story short we reached King's Cross in 5 minutes inside our six-and-a-half-hour schedule from Edinburgh; but delays en route had cost us fully 16 minutes in running. Without these we could have been more than *twenty minutes* early—with The Elizabethan. It was the last time I travelled with Sam Jenkins, and he retired soon afterwards.

Until the formation of British Railways in 1948 it was not everywhere customary to send an inspector when a visitor was riding on the footplate, except on the Western Region, as successor to the Great Western Railway, and it was at the time of the Interchange Trials following nationalization that I met one of the most amusing characters in the South of England. Danny Knight was chief locomotive inspector of the Southern, and he had to accompany the Bulleid air-smoothed 'Pacific' engines when they were on their away assignments. One of the trains they had to work was the 8.30 a.m. from Plymouth to Paddington, and this involved detaching a slip coach at Reading. Danny and his men were greatly intrigued by this, for at that time the Great Western had been the only railway still making use of slip coaches. This Reading slip was an awkward job, because it was preceded by the regular speed restriction at Reading West Junction, and one had then to run at continuing reduced speed through the platform, where the coach was detached.

The technique of slipping coaches was normally fairly simple. There was a separate guard in the slip coach and, at the appropriate moment, he operated a lever which uncoupled the coach, and the brake pipe closed again automatically. The vacuum brake reservoir on the slip coach would be fully exhausted, so that the slip guard had the facility of applying the brake gently and bringing the coach to rest at the correct place. But coming off the West of England line at Reading the driver had to brake to get his speed down to about 30 m.p.h., and then exhaust the brake system again, at once, so that the reservoir on the slip coach had the maximum degree of vacuum. Then he had to allow the train to 'roll' round the curve with the brakes off, while the slip was being detached. It was a tricky job. But the Southern men were good pupils, and made an excellent job of it first time. They continued up to Paddington and arrived punctually, and Danny Knight was on the platform chatting to his Western Region confreres when, out of the corner of his eye, he saw one of the ex-GWR diesel parcel vans running in at another platform.

Clutching his neighbour's arm he exclaimed 'Blimey, we must have been going at Reading. Here's our slip coach just arrived!'

Another category of inspectors, for whom I came to have a high regard, were the professional engineers, usually acting on behalf of overseas railway administrations, who visit manufacturing plants and scrutinize equipment before despatch. I had many dealings with one particular man during the later 1930s, when we had orders for many variations of the Neale's single line token instrument for Indian railways. He was a fly old character, instantly aware of anyone trying to pull the wool over his eyes. My boss of those days disliked him thoroughly, and put the job of contact with him on to me. We got on famously. He loved to talk, and from his long experience of Indian railways there was much to be learned from him. The climax of our own association came in the early summer of 1939, when we had a number of token instruments for the Madras and Southern Mahratta Railway ready for inspection. For some reason he could not immediately make the journey to Chippenham and, as the instruments were urgently needed, he asked me to do the inspection for him. 'Fine-tooth comb' did not describe the technique I used in going over those instruments! I should have hated to have let him down.

Another of these high-standing professionals that I came to know well dealt mainly with equipment for South Africa and South America. At one stage, just after the Second World War, I told him I was about to make application for transfer upwards from Associate Member to Full Member in the Institution of Mechanical Engineers. He said at once 'If you want a sponsor I'll sign your form; but mind you, the Institution's absolutely going to the dogs. They've just elected a *woman* as a member.' And the disdain, nay disgust, with which he emphasized the word boded ill for women's lib, as far as he had anything to do with it! He retired soon afterwards.

# 10 Glamour of the East

The United Nations Organization has a regional group known as the Economic Commission for Asia and the Far East, ECAFE for short, and at one time ECAFE had a railway subcommittee whose job it was to advise and help the developing countries of South East Asia on the latest techniques likely to help them. At a session of the railway subcommittee in Melbourne in June 1962 the need for increasing the carrying capacity of single line railways was discussed, and the delegations of the United Kingdom and France offered to assist ECAFE in the preparation of a textbook on the subject. Responsibility for the British share was taken by the United Kingdom Railway Advisory Service (UKRAS), an organization supported by British Railways and all the leading manufacturers of railway equipment; but from the end of that meeting in June 1962 things hung fire for a time. For one thing, after the first flush of enthusiasm the French showed little sign of wanting to co-operate, and it looked as though UKRAS was going to be left 'holding the baby'. What went on behind the scenes in the intervening twelve months I do not know, but in the early summer of 1963 Westinghouse instructed me to attend a meeting at the Charing Cross Hotel. By that time in my life my writing activities had become regarded as something of a Company asset! The Company had apparently agreed to give full support to the textbook project, and the end of that meeting found me appointed as editor.

It was an extraordinary project. Some twenty people, all experts in their respective fields, had attended that meeting. They were each charged with writing a learned contribution, and—heaven knows why!—I had been chosen to assemble it all together and build it into a comprehensive textbook, collecting all material necessary for illustration, and seeing the whole thing through the press. It had to be done among my ordinary duties as Chief Mechanical Engineer but, while I could not call on any of my technical staff for assistance, I had two excellent and willing clerks who were ready enough to put in overtime in helping to keep the purely clerical side of the job straight. As the contributions came in the paper work snowballed, but then another anxiety had begun to loom up. UKRAS had made arrangements for publication with a small man, quite unknown to me, in south-east London. I was invited to meet him at the Ministry of Transport, and was not impressed. It had been hoped to have the script ready for discussion and approval at the next meeting of the railway subcommittee of ECAFE, which would be held some time in 1964, and that we would go to press immediately after that; but there was something in the easy optimism of that printer-publisher and the speed he foresaw in getting the job through that increased my apprehension. Then it was announced that the 1964 ECAFE meeting would take place in October, in Bangkok, and the race was on to get the script ready in time. UKRAS asked that I should join the small British delegation to pilot the script through and, although at that time I was up to my eyes in ordinary work, Westinghouse decided that I should go.

The VC 10 took off from Karachi. We had not long finished dinner, and the night was going to be short. With my mind on the assignment that lay ahead, I slept but fitfully, and awoke before full daylight to see to the north one of the most extraordinary sights of my life. For there, about a hundred miles away, was the range of the Himalayas, a serried array extending far to left and right, with the rays of the rising sun touching on their jagged, snow-clad peaks. Below us there was not a vestige of colour. The sky had barely begun to change from dark purple to cloudless blue; but soon the vision was gone, and we were descending to the slum that then passed for an airport at Dum Dum, Calcutta. It was dull, steamy and oppressive, but I was glad to stretch my legs for the last time on this long run out from England and, as we rejoined the aircraft, next stop Bangkok, I thought again of the task that lay ahead. So there I was, flying east from Calcutta, feeling sick as much with apprehension as with lengthy travel, looking down on the forests of Burma, and then upon the incredible apparently waterlogged landscape of Thailand.

I need not dwell upon the events of the next six days: the plenary sessions, the committee work, the off-stage and back-stage gatherings, the entertainment and the entertaining, all in the heat and humidity of the Thai 'cool' season, which meant about 85 to 90 degrees in the shade, 100 per cent humidity, and two changes of clothes every day! Although we were talking of railways all the time, it was not until we had been a week in the country that I so much as *saw* a train. Getting approved the script of a book that eventually ran to 350 pages was desperately hard work, and after the final session on the Saturday morning at which it was approved—reluctantly on the part of at least two delegations—I could have slumped completely and given myself over to sleep and rest. But in our numerous goings and comings in Bangkok itself I had seen many alluring glimpses of temples and monuments and, tired as I was, I felt there would probably never come a second chance to see Bangkok; and so I spent the Saturday afternoon and the Sunday morning in some intensive sightseeing and photographing. Still, no trains!

Real business 'out the line' began on the Monday morning, when a special train was laid on for the delegates to take us, in three days of travelling, right down to Singapore. The previous week, however, had in its various ways taken its toll, and it was a somewhat jaded party that went aboard that special train. Not all the delegates to the conference came, and many of those who did retired early to the single-berth sleeping cabins with which we had all been provided. To many of my co-delegates the passing landscape, with its continuous alternation between dense jungle and rice fields, soon proved tedious, and they only emerged, rather sleepily, for meals and drinks. Jaded though I was personally, I soon found two of my other 'hats' planted firmly on my head. The chairman of the conference, Achava Kunjara, was Chief Mechanical Engineer of the Royal State Railways of Thailand. He had learned of my interest in all kinds of locomotives and took delight in plying me with details of everything we saw, while Banyong Saralamp, the Superintendent of Signals and Telegraphs, with whom Westinghouse was currently negotiating a contract for single line token instruments of the Indian Neale's type, insisted that I got down at every stopping station, went with him into the stationmaster's office, and inspected the equipment. The Thai railway officers had indeed turned out in force, and were making a positively gala occasion of it.

Our train was hauled by one of the latest German-built diesel-hydraulic locomotives, but otherwise everything else on this line to the south was hauled by steam, some American, some veteran British still going strong, and the latest—very smartly turned out—Japanese. All were wood-fired, and about this Achava Kunjara told me a good story. I had remarked upon the numerous small four-wheeled wagons piled high with sawn logs in sidings at many of the little stations deep in the jungle, and he laughed. Apparently the State Railways get an allocation of softwood from the Government for locomotive fuel, but at that time it was not nearly enough. By means that need not be disclosed, news of these shortages had been conveyed to the peasants in the jungle areas, and supplies of soft timber, nicely cut to size, began to appear as if by magic at the stations. It was then an easy matter to load them on to these little wagons and attach them to the next goods train going in the right direction, for the attention of a more than grateful shed master. These logs burn very rapidly, and a tender stacked to its maximum capacity will take a locomotive barely 100 miles. The workings have to be arranged with many changes, so that a locomotive always arrives at a place where fuel is available after 70 or 80 miles of running.

The line to the south is all single-tracked and unfenced and, although it is fully equipped with token apparatus and telegraphs, the engine-drivers have always to be on the look-out for obstructions. They did not seem to be troubled in Thailand by the larger and more dangerous of wild animals, such as the tigers and elephants that at one time used to get in the way in Malaya. It was more the fearsome-looking, but utterly placid, domestic water buffalo, which sometimes strays from its lawful pastures and takes a leisurely walk along the railway, that concerned them. We had an experience of this on our first day out from Bangkok. We were ambling pleasantly along at about 40 m.p.h. when suddenly the brakes went on hard and we stopped. Looking out, I saw a water buffalo lying asleep right in the centre of the track. On the second day out Achava Kunjara invited me to ride on the footplate, and I was able to see to better advantage, and photograph, this fascinating metre-gauge ribbon of a railway, making its way through tropical jungle. The lineside villages were little more than shanty settlements; the rivers we crossed were turgid and muddy. Away from the temples and palaces of Bangkok the eastern glamour consisted in remoteness.

On the afternoon of the second day we came to the frontier station of Padang Besar, and exchanged our Thai diesel-hydraulic locomotives for a British-built Malayan diesel-electric. The overcast, thundery weather that had clouded the skies and dulled the colouring of the landscape had cleared by this time and it was blazing hot. We were getting nearer to the equator. There was practically no twilight and, by 6.30 p.m., after the sun had set in a cloudless sky, it was quite dark. At Prai, the ferry port opposite to Penang Island, we were to change from the Thai train that had been our 'hotel' for two days into the Malayan night express for Kuala Lumpur. It had been a comfortable journey for, without air-conditioning, we had had no trouble from dust while travelling, and had been able to keep the windows open. But when we reached Prai, although it was late, the night was still and hot, and we revelled in the freshness and cool of the beautiful air-conditioned sleepers to which we transferred. Although running on the metre gauge, these fine British-built cars are as wide as anything on the home railways and sumptuously appointed. With the additional cars added for our party it made up an immense train of twenty coaches, but this was taken without difficulty by a single diesel-electric locomotive of 1,500 horsepower.

I shall never forget that journey. I saw nothing of the Malayan countryside, alas, but what I did experience, in too full measure, was the effectiveness of the air-conditioning. The fragrant coolness that was so welcome when we entered at Prai turned to a chilly feeling. I snuggled under the bedclothes in a way I had not done since leaving England, but to no avail. After the heat of the day the chill in that sleeping berth was becoming lethal. There was nothing for it but to stuff up the ingress of air with spare underclothes. Then I had a comfortable night. Since leaving Bangkok we had all been travelling in the most informal of dress and, with the prospect of a hot day 'out the line' around Kuala Lumpur, we were arrayed similarly when the night express drew into that remarkable oriental station around breakfast time. Imagine our horror when, waiting on the platform in all their party clothes, were the General Manager and his full entourage. Describing how we dashed back into our sleepers, put on collars and ties and emerged in a semblance of formality takes longer than the time it took us!

Apart from a marvellous afternoon of non-railway sightseeing and a 'sundowner', as they call them in Africa, at the General Manager's residence, the highlight of our visit to Kuala Lumpur was a tour of the railway works at Sentul, where all activities of the Chief Mechanical Engineer's department were concentrated. The truth of the old tag 'It's a small world' was brought home by something that happened at the end of our tour at Sentul. I had been conducted round by the very charming acting CME, a Sikh by the name of Dalip Singh, and a very fine mechanical engineer; and with one or two others we went at length into his office. On the wall were some group photographs, and sitting in the middle of some of these was an Englishman whom I recognised as my next-door-but-one neighbour in Batheaston. We had not long previously moved to our present home, and had met him no more than briefly up till then. He was the last European to be Chief Mechanical Engineer of the Malayan Railways. Dalip Singh was delighted. He said 'When you get home tell Jim Ball we're trying to run the job as he taught us,' which I thought was a very charming appreciation.

When Jim Ball first went to Sentul as Works Manager, the place was little more than a heap of ruins. In the closing stages of the Second World War, during the liberation of Malaya, a locomotive, carriage and wagon works serving such a far-flung railway system was a military target of the first importance, and it had been treated accordingly by the Allied air forces. In the rebuilding of it, one of the most important considerations was the almost inevitably impending change from steam to diesel traction, and very great care was taken to segregate the workshops that would deal with the 'dirty' steam and the 'clean' diesel. The introduction of the diesels was made with great deliberation, with the result that the Malayan Railways suffered little or nothing of the teething troubles experienced in Great Britain through the intermingling of steam and diesel facilities in the same sheds. In Malaya the diesels were of course put on to the prestige jobs, and a suggestion was made that the nice new locomotives should be named after the flowers of the Malayan countryside. The local humorists pounced upon this, and a cartoon appeared in one of the leading national newspapers showing a diesel driver being ribbed as a 'pansy' by one of his steam colleagues!

Mention of Sikhs naturally leads me on to India which, other than passing through, I did not visit until more than ten years later. But before I tell of some of my experiences 'out the line' in that amazing subcontinent there is more to be related about that textbook, which was far from finished when I returned to England from Bangkok with the slightly amended script in my luggage. The mechanics of publication were quickly completed, and all went off to that rather mysterious 'publisher'. Then a great silence fell over the whole enterprise. Not a word came in reply. I wrote to enquire if he had received my weighty package; still no reply. I telephoned because the business of proof correction was going to take some time, and I wanted to be sure I was not loaded up with other spare-time activities when that job came along. 'He would ring me up.' Another fortnight passed. Christmas was near. I managed to catch him personally on the telephone; he said that the printer was being somewhat 'coy', to use his own expression, about a likely proof date. After all the euphemistic words before I went to Bangkok, I began to get suspicious. However, I let the festive season pass, and it was not until January was nearing its end, with still not a line on paper, that I confided my fears to Bernard Strouts, the deputy chairman of UKRAS. Another week or so passed, and then the incredible story came out.

Our precious script, written by seventeen specialists, which I had travelled half way round the world to get approved, was impounded; impounded by the printers as a hostage against the debts of our so-called publisher, and in a domestic fracas at the latter's home all the photographs I had collected for illustrating the book had been torn up! Well here was a pretty kettle of fish. The chairman of UKRAS shrugged his shoulders and was apparently prepared to accept the demise of the text book there and then; but the loss of prestige to British Railways and British industry would have been incalculable had the misfortune been allowed to submerge the whole project, and with Bernard Strouts' agreement I began to make some enquiries among my own friends in the publishing world. With great good fortune one, who had taken some of my work and I knew to be sound, was due in London in the next few days. I made an appointment with him and told him the whole dismal story. He was interested, and a meeting was arranged at the Ministry of Transport at which an agreement was concluded. It was never vouchsafed to me what sort of an agreement UKRAS had with the other character, but we never got our typescript or photographs back, and I had to start collecting illustrations all over again. We were on firm ground this time, however, and the textbook was eventually published about sixteen months after the conference at Bangkok. It had the simple title *Single Line Railways*.

Nearly ten years later, in Madras, I called on my friend S. M. Gauri Shanker, Chief Signal and Telecommunications Engineer of the Southern Railway in India. I had met him first when he was visiting the Westinghouse works in Chippenham, and in his own office he greeted me. 'Well, we've taken your advice about single line railways, and I should like you to autograph the book.' I had not the time nor the heart to tell him how that book was very nearly stillborn. I had been down in the far south of India, in the province that used to be known as Travancore and is now called Kerala, travelling on the single-tracked metre-gauge line from Cochin to Trivandrum. Kerala is the most densely populated part of India. This may be surprising but, while there are dense concentrations of people in the north in the great cities, intermediately, as I saw when I travelled by the former Oudh and Rohilkund main line between Varanasi and Lucknow, there are very lengthy stretches that are entirely pastoral. Down in Kerala traffic on the single line railway between Cochin and Trivandrum is reaching saturation point. At Cochin it links up with a broad-gauge line, and the bold step is being taken of converting it.

Because of the great distances involved, and because time was not on my side, I went to Cochin by air and, flying at no great height on a wonderfully clear day, had a marvellous view of the country below. It could well be described as exotic. Except where the rivers made a winding course, and where there were sandy lagoons along the coast, the whole landscape was, or seemed to be, completely covered in palms, of a most brilliant green. The railway people were there to meet the arrival of the plane from Bombay, and we all boarded an inspection saloon on the rear of a mixed train for the south. It is always a fascinating experience to travel at the extreme rear-end of a train and, through a coach-wide 'picture' window, watch the track recede. I have done it at up to 110 m.p.h. on an inspection special between London and Liverpool, but to roll placidly along through this brilliant tropical landscape surpassed all. I saw where the track formation had been widened and longer sleepers put in to carry the rails of the 5 ft 6 in. gauge. When the time came for changeover, things were going to be much simpler than in that historic classic of gauge conversion on the Great Western Railway in England, in 1892, when more than a hundred miles of Brunel's 7 ft road were changed to the standard 4 ft 8½ in. in a single weekend. Then they took one rail up and slewed it into the new position. In Kerala the broad (5 ft 6 in.) gauge road will be laid with new and heavier rails, outside the existing metre-gauge track. If the traffic develops as expected this converted line may even be electrified.

My earliest association with Indian Railways came a very long time before I actually visited the country. As a young draughtsman I assisted in the design of some of the special equipment for the re-signalling of the celebrated Victoria Terminus station in Bombay, then headquarters of the Great Indian Peninsula Railway. This was indeed the very birthplace of railways in India, because it was from Bombay that the first Indian train ran in 1853. When I was there soon after Christmas in 1975 the officers of the present Central Railway, successor to the GIPR, had much to show me, and out on the line at 'VT', as everyone calls the great station, I was delighted to find that some of the equipment for which I made drawings more than forty-five years ago was still working. But the greatest railway sights anywhere near Bombay are the Ghat Inclines and, on an express train bound for the Deccan, I once again had the privilege of a 'front seat' in the driver's cab of the electric locomotive. In India the Western Ghats provided one of the classic problems facing railway engineers in different parts of the world, where a mountain range of exceptional severity had to be surmounted. I have written elsewhere in this book of the Lötschberg line in Switzerland, of the Semmering, and even of the short, though equally severe, Lickey Incline in the West Midlands of England. The Western Ghats had the same physical characteristics of a tumbled, exceedingly rugged, and confusing welter of escarpments on the face of a chain of mountains that stretched for hundreds of miles, not far inland and parallel to the west coast of India. The situation faced in the surveys, and in searching for the best way up the mountainside, was not unlike that of the Semmering, except that construction had to be carried out in a sweltering tropical atmosphere and amid the torrential and yearly visitations of the monsoon. In the climb up the Bhor Ghat, on the main line from Bombay to Poona and across India to Madras, there is an ascent at around 1 in 40 for fifteen miles, and this has provided a problem in operation ever since the line was opened.

In the Imperial days Indian railway practice was based largely on that of Great Britain, and one similarity was in the standardization of the vacuum automatic brake in preference to the Westinghouse air brake. In the discussions following the many lectures I have given on various aspects of railway operation I have frequently been asked which I think is the better of the two brakes; and I have nearly always replied by putting on the most commercial of my 'hats' and saying that we—Westinghouse that is—were prepared to make either, as we did of course, in large quantities. On a fast running, moderately graded line both brakes can be used to full advantage, and the magnificent records of the British companies in steam days were all achieved with vacuum-fitted stock. But, without becoming partisan or making odious comparisons, I can say that the air brake has it every time when it comes to working long and steep gradients. The great problem of the Ghats is not of providing power to get up, but of controlling heavy trains safely on the way down, with the vacuum brake.

I had a wonderful day 'out the line' with my friends of the Central Railway. The weather was glorious, not too hot, and from the driver's cab of the electric locomotive the rugged, rather bewildering nature of the country reminded me very much of the Semmering line, except that in Austria one did not see members of the public milling nonchalantly about on the track! We made no speed records on the way up, and with electric locomotives front and rear our speed varied between 22 and 28 m.p.h. At the summit, at Lonavla station, I climbed down, for there was much to see. An inspection trolley was waiting to take us about a mile further east to where westbound freight trains are examined before making the descent of the Bhor Ghat. Inspection trolleys, or 'bogeys' as they are sometimes called, are always rather fun to ride. There is immense satisfaction in going through a line in a little petrol-driven 'buggy', classified as an 'express passenger train'; but this one up at Lonavla was different. It was purely a trolley pushed by four men, though once it was fairly moving on level track they began to run, and we got along at quite a fair speed. So we came to the lengthy sidings where westbound freight trains are examined. Every brake cylinder is individually tested, and plenty of spares are kept on hand in case one or two need to be replaced. We went back to Lonavla station in time for me to ride down the big hill to Karjak on the leading locomotive of a heavy freight train.

The weight of the train was given as 1,682 tons, not heavy by modern standards in Australia and North America; but working vacuum, not Westinghouse, the greatest care is needed with such a load, and two additional diesel-electric locomotives were coupled ahead of the road locomotive, a British-built electric, to provide additional brake power. Going down the hill I rode the leading diesel, the driver of which was in charge of the train. We made a brake check at Khandala catch siding, and then came to Thakurwadi. These catch sidings are designed to divert wagons, or a whole train in the event of a runaway, and at Thakurwadi there is a most spectacular one, extending for 1,325 yards right up one of the mountain sides, on a very steep gradient. It would make a dramatic setting for some fantastic film scenario involving a runaway train! The cautious nature of our descent is emphasized by the fact that it took us 70 minutes to negotiate the 17 miles down from Lonavla.

Of all the varied sights I have seen on Indian railways none can surpass that of the electric trains running into Bombay and Calcutta at the height of the morning suburban rush. The people pack into the carriages like sardines, while those who cannot get through the entrances hang in a cluster round each door. These doors are sliding, but no one attempts to close them, and an approaching train presents an amazing sight, with these clusters of white-clad commuters hanging on throughout the train. The only variation is at the 'ladies only' compartments where the 'clusters', instead of being white, are made up of brilliant coloured saris and draperies flying in the wind! To see three such trains arrive simultaneously at the Howrah station, Calcutta, and watch a total of about 8,500 people disgorge into the concourse and *across the tracks* in a single human torrent is one of the railway sights of the world.

Crowding was not confined to the commuter trains on my visit to Howrah. With my friends of the Eastern and the South Eastern Railways—successors of the East Indian and the Bengal Nagpur companies—I went out along the line to see the diesel shops, and then to the steam running shed. Photographs of our party were being taken from all angles. They had discovered that the following day was my seventieth birthday, and found an old 0–6–0 goods engine of the same age and photographed us together; and then as many as could climb aboard got on to a diesel, to face the camera. But this was nothing to our return trip from the steam shed to the station. They evidently thought that an old gentleman of 70 had done enough walking for one morning, and provided a lift back on a 'WP' streamlined 'Pacific' that was about to leave, to pick up its train. All would have been well if only my guides and the photographer had come too; but seven or eight other people were all ready to hitch a lift, and I counted fourteen beside the driver and fireman, on or around that engine when we finally backed down from the shed. Had our camera man not been encased in the jam inside the cab he could have secured the railway picture of the century.

# 11 Doing the 'Ton'

'. . . Then you can go and break your bloody neck!' Churchward's homely words to Inspector Flewellyn, which presaged the first attainment of 100 m.p.h. by a British train, probably came nearer to actuality in the hair-raising speeds run over the curves of the South Devon line on that memorable 9 May, 1904, than in the dash down from Whiteball Tunnel to Taunton, where the 'ton' was actually reached. Speeds of 70 to 75 m.p.h. on the curves between Brent and Newton Abbot were far more dangerous than 100 or 102 on the relatively straight length from Whiteball Tunnel, which we sometimes call the Wellington Bank. So it was also on the Invitation Run of the Coronation Scot on 29 June 1937. It was not the 114 m.p.h. on the straight between Betley Road and Basford Hall, but the curves into Crewe, that constituted the risk; and the risk on some of the LNER speed ventures was in wrecking the valve gear of the locomotive. Far otherwise was my only other personal experience of 100 m.p.h. running in the years before the Second World War.

My wife and I were travelling south from Edinburgh on the newly-instituted Coronation express of the LNER in the summer of 1937. It was a much heavier train than the first Gresley 'streamliner', the Silver Jubilee of 1935, and its haulage demanded something quite near to the maximum capacity of the brilliant 'A4' streamlined 'Pacific' engines. With the introduction of these fast streamlined trains a new departure had been made, for publicity purposes, in finishing them in distinctive colours. Thus the Silver Jubilee *was* silver coloured, and the Coronation was in a two-tone colour scheme of Cambridge and Garter blue.

With the introduction of the Coronation the most ambitious locomotive working yet tried on the LNER began. In each direction one engine worked through between London and Edinburgh. A second blue engine stood by, as reserve, until the 'flyer' had departed, while the fifth engine was available as a spare. But it was the through working, over 392¾ miles at streamlined express speed with a train nearly 50 per cent heavier than the Silver Jubilee, that provided the tax. It is true that since 1928 the Flying Scotsman had been run non-stop between London and Edinburgh, but that was on a much slower schedule. The major problem with the Coronation was coal supply. The tenders carried 9 tons, which allowed for an average consumption of 50 lbs per mile. For such sustained fast running this did not allow a great deal of margin, even with such economical engines as the 'A4' 'Pacifics', and if the weather was bad and strong cross winds were encountered, the crew could be in real trouble. Indeed, on more than one wintry occasion the southbound train had to stop at Hitchin to take on more coal.

But what is all this leading up to? How about 'doing the ton'? Well, on the occasion when we were travelling a very careful, experienced and resolute driver from Gateshead shed, Walker by name, had taken over from his Edinburgh confrère at Newcastle, to run the 268¼ miles to King's Cross in the scheduled 237 minutes, an average of 68 m.p.h. It was the first time he had ever worked the train, and he had the *Commonwealth of Australia* engine, No. 4491. With the diligence of a first-class driver he had slightly over-emphasized some of the regular speed restrictions, and from Selby southwards, for about an hour, he was running 1½ to 2 minutes behind time. But, once we had taken the 20-mile rise from Newark to Stoke Tunnel, ahead of us lay the supreme racing ground of all England—another 20 miles of almost perfect, superbly maintained downhill track. It was not unduly steep, and in fact it tapered out to dead level by the time Peterborough was about 5 miles ahead: a place for record-making, if ever there was one!

We passed Newark at 80 m.p.h. The engine was not being pressed. The careful driver had his eye on the coal supply, and had in mind memories of what befell *Silver Fox* on the southbound Jubilee when she was pushed a little too hard in some trials about a year previously. He and his fireman had the *Commonwealth of Australia* in a beautiful balanced condition, steaming at an almost constant rate, with the valve-gear adjustment giving about 80 to 82 m.p.h. on level track. On that lengthy rise from Newark speed gradually fell away till my final stop watch readings gave 64½ m.p.h. over the summit, and I remember remarking to my wife 'Now what's going to happen?' I learned afterwards from Walker that he did not touch the controls. He allowed the engine to find its own pace downhill, and we were soon going like a positive whirlwind. My wife went out into the vestibule, and remained there, standing without touching a door or handle for support, while in 3 miles from the summit we were doing 85, in another 5 miles we had reached 100, and for the next 10 miles we *averaged* 104½ m.p.h. During this time the speed lay entirely between 104 and 106 m.p.h., and all the time the riding in the train was as smooth and quiet as if we were sliding over ice.

Technically it was a most important exposition, because it showed the natural maximum of a skilfully handled, well tuned up engine; and I can only say that we continued from Peterborough to make fast and punctual running over the rest of the journey to London.

Nearly seventeen years later I had an engine pass to ride the Tees–Tyne Pullman, from Newcastle to King's Cross. After the end of the Second World War the Eastern group managements were constantly anxious to restore the speed and prestige of the London–Leeds and London–Newcastle business services; but for a variety of reasons this was not possible, and the best that could be done was the introduction of reasonably fast Pullman trains. The Tees–Tyne Pullman, as its name implied, served Newcastle and, through connections at Darlington, the Tees-side industrial complex. From Darlington a non-stop run was made over the 232¼ miles to King's Cross in 230 minutes. This average of just over 60 m.p.h. was a rather pale shade of what the Silver Jubilee used to do, with its average of 70 m.p.h., but it was the best that could be regularly scheduled in the 1950s. The total load of the eight Pullmans was almost exactly the same as that of the nine-coach streamlined Coronation of 1937, 330 tons. The engine was one of the 'A4' streamliners, *Woodcock*, and I was pleased to find that the driver was Bill Hoole. He was one of that breed of resolute enginemen who are prepared to run hard when occasion demands, and always ready to 'have a go'; but he was rather abashed on this occasion, when he found that Inspector Dixon, of King's Cross, was also going to ride with us. Dixon sensed from the glint in his eye that Hoole was out to give his visitor 'something to write about', as he said afterwards, and on the platform at Newcastle said 'Now Bill, you know all the speed limits, don't you?' 'Limit's 110, isn't it?' 'Now Bill you know perfectly well its ninety'!

The official line maximum certainly was 90 m.p.h. at that time, but on certain stretches where the track was in good shape authority raised no objection to a little bending of the rules, if a driver was making up lost time. At one of my many pleasant meetings with E. D. Trask, the Motive Power Superintendent of Eastern Region, when we were talking about high maximum speeds, he said he 'would not bat an eyelid' at an excess of 5 per cent, and would not worry much about 10 per cent on the better stretches of line. So, with such a driver as Hoole and a first-class engine, I looked forward to some interesting work south of Grantham. As it happened there was an unexpected treat in store for me before that. We left Darlington on our non-stop run to London, and I soon saw from the footplate how an 'A4' could develop its own natural hurricane stride, on a magnificent stretch south of Northallerton where the gradient is only very slightly in favour of the engine. The regulator was fairly wide

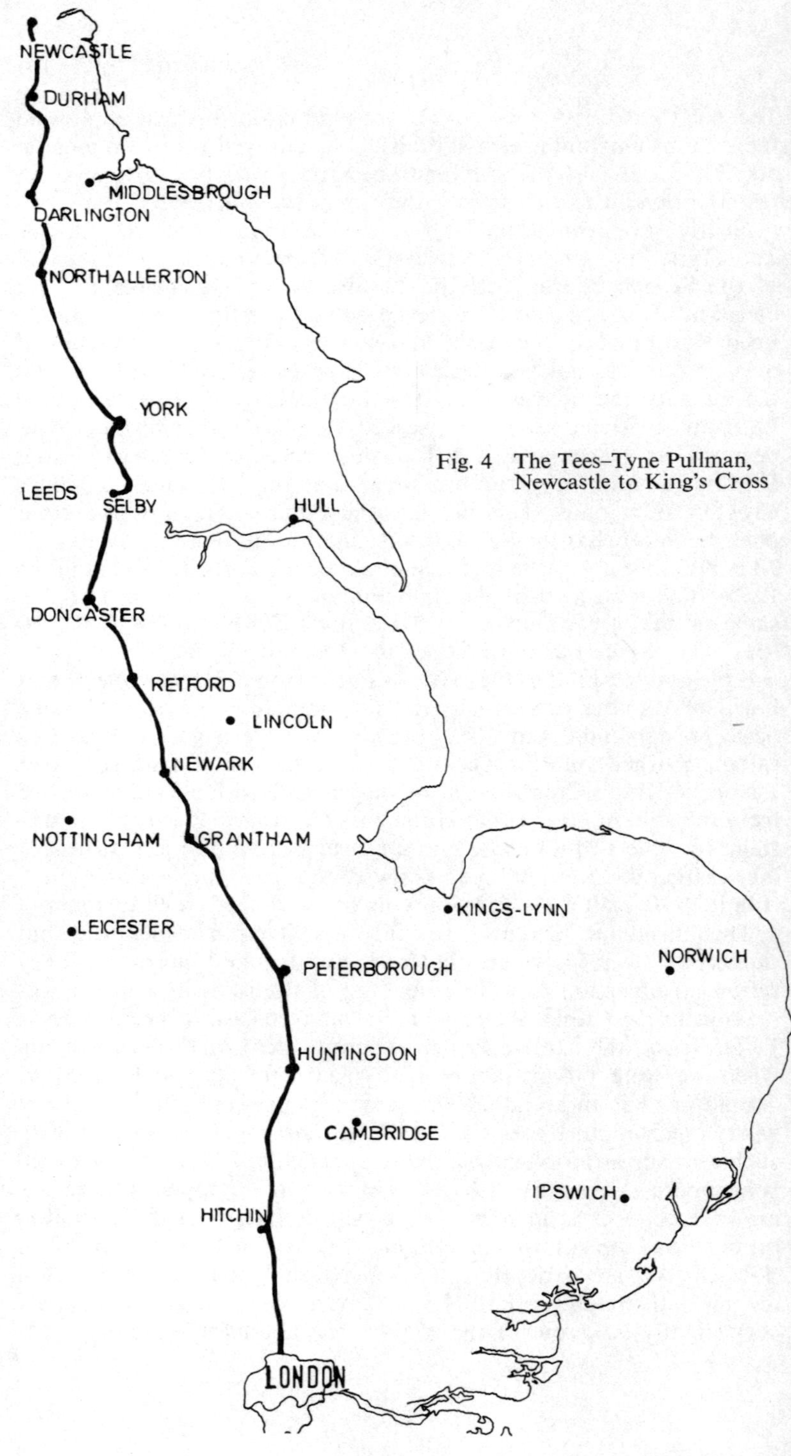


Fig. 4 The Tees–Tyne Pullman, Newcastle to King's Cross

open, but on a steam locomotive this does not mean you are going 'flat out'—far from it. What matters is the point at which the valves are cutting off steam supply to the cylinders in each piston stroke, and here *Woodcock* had almost the minimum setting, a cut-off at 15 per cent of the stroke. This was ideal, economic working on an 'A4' and it gave us an average speed of 87 m.p.h. for 21 miles, with a maximum of 89 m.p.h. The 'A4s' were always smooth and elegant engines to ride, and this was an immaculate exhibition.

Then we were stopped by signal in York station, and, on getting the road once again, to my surprise and delight Inspector Dixon invited me to drive for a bit. The booked point-to-point times over the next 40 miles did not demand such fast running as that we had just made south of Northallerton, and while I also linked the valves up to give 15 per cent cut-off I did not have the regulator open so wide. While Bill Hoole's previous adjustment had given a pressure of 200 lbs per sq. in. in the steam entering the cylinders, mine gave only 160; but it took us merrily along on the level stretch south of Selby at 75 m.p.h. I eased down to run through the complicated junction areas on both sides of Doncaster, and having taken *Woodcock* over the 32¼ miles from the restart at York in just under 33 minutes I handed the controls back to Hoole. He did not immediately take the regulator himself, but took the shovel instead. It was not unusual on these London–Newcastle through workings for driver and fireman to exchange duties for half an hour or so. The firemen on those top-link jobs were all first-class enginemen and passed as drivers, and a break in the middle of the run gave a short respite, and if they felt like it the chance of a bite.

From my resumed seat on the right-hand side of the cab I soon noticed that Bill Hoole was not just keeping things going for his mate. He was carefully and assiduously building up a much bigger fire than had previously sufficed. I remembered the glint in his eye on the platform at Newcastle, and by now Newark and the beginning of that 20-mile rise to Stoke Tunnel were less than half an hour's run ahead of us. With Hoole still building up, and memories of that exciting run on the Coronation back in 1937, I began to wonder what might happen after we topped the summit. If anything was afoot the prelude to it was much more restrained. Whereas on that pre-war journey we had come down to the Trent Valley at 96 m.p.h. and eased to nothing less than 80 through Newark, now we had not exceeded 82 m.p.h. at Crow Park, and were required by contemporary restrictions to reduce to 60 m.p.h. through Newark. This latter restriction we obeyed precisely. Then Hoole and his fireman changed to their normal duties, and he began to open up. Over the one easier pitch on that long upward slope we reached no less than

75 m.p.h., and on the last 5 miles of the gradient the speed fell to 65½ m.p.h.—one mile per hour *faster* than on the Coronation.

Once we were over the top the acceleration was terrific. Hoole was obviously going for that '110' with which he had ribbed Inspector Dixon, and Dixon himself came over to my side of the cab, looking over my shoulder at the speeds I was rapidly jotting down as my stop watch clocked the whizzing mileposts. Nearing Little Bytham, where the engine of the Coronation, finding her own pace, had got to 97 m.p.h., we had already topped the hundred, and we still swiftly accelerated. Then Dixon went across and quietly laid a hand on Hoole's shoulder, and without a word between them the driver eased the regulator back considerably, and at Essendine we were down to 90 m.p.h. The maximum speed was 103½ m.p.h. and I must say I was glad when it was over. It was not that the riding was rough or alarming, but a cross-wind set up a perfect whirlwind of coal dust inside the cab. I never wore goggles on the footplate in England, but much more of those conditions and I should have had to close my eyes. The reduction in speed from '100-plus' to 86–7 m.p.h. made all the difference. But I had clocked another 'ton', as it proved later the highest speed I have ever notched up on a steam locomotive footplate.

The mid-1950s were a time of awakening in Great Britain to the priceless heritage of the historical railway relics we then had, and a desire, not only by connoisseurs but also by serving railwaymen, to make the most of them. Of this there was no more remarkable a case than that of the *City of Truro*. Since withdrawal from regular service that famous engine had been in the care of the York Railway Museum, discreetly moved to a place of greater safety during the Second World War. In 1957, however, the Western Region had in R. F. Hanks a Chairman who was not just a former apprentice in the locomotive department at Swindon, but one who throughout his long and distinguished career in the motor industry had remained an out-and-out steam locomotive 'fan' and a Great Western supporter to his fingertips. And it was in 1957, through his interest and enthusiasm, that the *City of Truro* was extracted from York Railway Museum, brought to Swindon and given a superb refit. She was to run the rails again, not merely as a mobile museum piece, but as a revenue-earning engine, hauling special trains. Moreover she was restored to the highly colourful livery of the nineteenth century, with light red underframes and wheel centres, and more elaborate lining than that used later. Outwardly she differed in only two respects from her appearance at the time she became the first British locomotive, and in all probability the first world locomotive, to 'do the ton'. In 1957 she retained the large copper-capped chimney with which she went to York in 1932, and the top feed apparatus on either side of her safety valve bonnet.

After some preliminary running, during which her gay turnout caused great interest and admiration in the Swindon, Bath and Bristol area, it was announced that she was to work a Sunday seaside excursion, from Swindon to Kingswear. This was to be no leisurely 'doddle'; the 80 miles between Bristol and Teignmouth were to be run non-stop in each direction, and I was to have the privilege of a footplate pass. So confident were the running inspectors in the staying power and speed worthiness of the restored engine that Will Andress, then the chief locomotive inspector of Western Region, confided to me that on the return journey he was really going to have a go down Wellington Bank, where the '100' had been reached in 1904. This was thrilling news. The only snag was that the excursion proved so popular, with heavy advance bookings, that the traffic department had to run a train of eight coaches. The Ocean Mail of 9 May 1904 had a load of five vans, heavily freighted, 148 tons in all. The 1957 equivalent to this in passenger stock would have been five. Andress was a bit disappointed, but did not give up the idea of making a record.

On the outward journey the engine performed like a perfect lady. She handled the 265-ton train easily and to time. My wife and daughter had come for the ride, and we got down to Kingswear with plenty of time to take the ferry across to Dartmouth and spend a lazy afternoon on that delightful waterfront. Over the very steep gradients of the branch line from Newton Abbot we had one of the powerful 2–6–2 tank engines to help in the haulage and, although by mutual arrangement this latter engine did most of the work, the *City of Truro*, for decorative purposes, was leading. Andress was anxious that everything should be in perfect trim for the fast return run, non-stop, from Teignmouth to Bristol. It had been a lovely day, and by evening the weather still held, fine and clear; and it was in the keenest anticipation that we got away from Teignmouth. Round the picturesque red cliffs—past Dawlish and Starcross—beside the estuary of the river Exe—then slowly through Exeter St David's station; then we were away in earnest up the Exe Valley and towards the Blackdown Ridge, marking the county boundary between Devon and Somerset.

The *City of Truro* was really working now. With a load heavy for a locomotive of her vintage, she was equalling, uphill, the speeds of the Cornish Riviera Express and the modern Ocean Mails, hauled by 'Castle' or 'King' engines. But while this work was grand in itself the chances of 'doing the ton' down the Wellington Bank, as

Andress had fully intended, began to recede in my mind. In 1904, with that five-coach mail train, the Whiteball summit had been topped at 52 m.p.h. and acceleration thereafter was very swift. With a load of 265 tons, instead of 148, we could not hope to match such brilliant uphill speed, and on the last two miles up to the tunnel where the gradient stiffens to the quite steep inclination of 1 in 115 this resuscitated 'museum piece' did remarkably well not to fall below 39 m.p.h.

Then, over the summit, and as on that occasion 53 years earlier she was allowed to run. There was no attempt to force an exceptional or unnatural speed out of her. To do so would have been the height of folly. But she 'flew' all the same and, where previously she had swept up from 52 to the 'ton', she now went from 39 up to 84 m.p.h., and dashed on down towards Taunton with little slackening off, until we had to slow down to cross on to the Bristol line, by Taunton station. It was a thrilling experience to ride this stately old engine at such a splendid speed. It is interesting to speculate whether, had we conveyed a lighter load, she would have given us the 'ton'. Calculations of horsepower show pretty clearly that with a load of only 150 tons we could have gone over Whiteball summit at the 1904 speed of 52 m.p.h., but the rest is only conjecture. I know Will Andress would love to have tried; but the opportunity never came again!

In the last ten years running at 100 m.p.h. on British Railways has become commonplace on the part of the largest and most powerful diesel and electric locomotives, and I have some vivid experiences to relate in my chapter on the Electric Scots; but just now I must tell how they were 'doing the ton' in France when I went from Paris to the Côte d'Azur in the summer of 1971. Although it has been surpassed in maximum speed by some of the trains on the former Paris–Orleans Railway, the Mistral is still one of the most glamourous of all French express trains. Its very name breathes the spirit of breathless haste, for it refers to the tremendous wind that sweeps down from the Alps across the level lands of the Rhone delta with such fury sometimes as to uproot trees and other vegetation. The main line of the former Paris, Lyons and Mediterranean Railway is carried across this country between Avignon and Marseilles on a very long, shallow embankment, extending for more than 40 miles, and this has always presented certain problems in operation.

Some seventy years ago observers who did not know what climatic conditions existed sometimes in the Rhone delta were apt to poke fun at the idea of the PLM compound 4–4–0s having a modicum of streamlining at the front, because the speeds then scheduled were not very high; but there was no publicity stunting about the design of those engines. The French *cheminots* called them *les machines coupe vent*—in other words, the wind-cutters—and those strangely-shaped fronts certainly helped when they were battling against the Mistral. One of these engines is preserved in the French Railway Museum at Mulhouse, and it is a most dramatic thing to look upon. Right across this exposed stretch of line thick hedges of cypress trees have been grown on both sides of the track, so much so that the view across the country as seen from the train is completely obscured for most of the way, and one cannot see a great deal more when riding in the driver's cab. But from the Mistral itself to the Mistral train—one of the celebrated Trans-Europe Express (TEE) services. To see it at its fastest is to travel on its first stage to the south, between Paris and Dijon, over which 195¼ miles only 138 minutes were allowed when I travelled in 1971. Even this fast average of nearly 85 m.p.h. from start to stop does not give a true picture of the speed maintained over the greater part of this distance, nor of the tremendous power output involved.

The modern French electric trains are not only very fast, but also very heavy, and when I rode in the engine cab from Paris to Dijon we had no fewer than fourteen of the very latest *grand confort* coaches, making a load of 715 tons. The great locomotives of the 'CC 6500' class which are capable of a maximum continuous output of 7,500 horsepower, more than double the power of the largest British diesels, are beautiful machines to ride, and the driver and inspector as usual made me very welcome. It was, however, a little time on this particular journey before we could really get going. There was a long slowing for permanent way work before even we got abreast of the enormous marshalling yards at Villeneuve St Georges, and we were running 3 minutes late before we were 9 miles out of Paris. We had our first taste of the 'ton' at Lieusaint, but speed had to be moderated frequently when we were running through the Forest of Fontainebleau, where there are many curves. It was all very exciting, however. The track is heavily canted on these curves, and we approached some of them at a breathtaking speed, with the locomotive heeling over on the transition, and taking them without a tremor. The first few times when this happened, at speeds of 90 to 95 m.p.h., fairly made me hold my breath!

It was after Montereau was passed, 48¾ miles out of Paris, still 1½ minutes late, although in no more than 39½ minutes from the start, that we really settled down to a long sustained spell of continuous high-speed running. Up the valley of the river Yonne the track is much straighter and for the next 80 minutes our speed lay entirely between 93 and 100 m.p.h. By this time I had become used to the great speed, and it was only when we passed other trains going towards Paris, or overtook slower ones, that I sensed again how fast we *were* going. In metric quantities the speed limit is 160 kilometres per hour—exactly the 'hundred' in miles per hour—and this was never even fractionally exceeded. We covered the 47½ miles from Montereau to the important junction of Laroche at an average speed of 98½ m.p.h., and were then exactly on time. The track had been practically level up to now in the aggregate, but at Laroche there begins a gradual climb towards the Côte d'Or mountains, and in another 82½ miles there is a difference in height above sea level of 1,044 ft. At the summit, just before the entrance to the tunnel at Blaisy Bas, the altitude is 1,324 ft, higher than all British main line summits with the sole exception of Druimuachdar Pass, on the Perth–Inverness line. It was hard to imagine we had climbed so high.

Yet it is no exaggeration to say that the long and steepening rise from Laroche made little difference to the whirlwind progress of the Mistral. The driver skilfully adjusted the controls to keep the speed practically constant, taking more and more current from the overhead line. We were getting slightly ahead of time and the needle of the speedometer was kept on the 155 kilometres per hour mark. The average speeds show this performance in a remarkable light. The gradients, although steepening, do not become severe until Les Laumes is passed, and the average speed over the 63¼ miles from Laroche to this station was 95½ m.p.h.; then, over the last 19¼ miles, where the gradient stiffens finally to 1 in 125, the same as on the southbound ascent to Shap, the average speed was 94¾ m.p.h. Let not those fourteen *grand confort* coaches be forgotten either, that we were lifting in such powerful style. Despite the slow start out of Paris and the fact that it was not until after Montereau that we could really settle down to 100 m.p.h. running, the 179 miles from the start to Blaisy Bas had taken only 30 seconds over the level two hours—an average of just over 89 m.p.h.; and the 160 miles from Lieusaint to the summit had taken only a few seconds over 100 minutes, a splendid average of nearly 96 m.p.h.—for 160 miles on end. This is rather technical, but it is fitting to get technical for a few minutes to pay tribute to the brains that have gone to the making of such achievements in modern travel.

This was certainly 'doing the ton', or something very near to it, with a vengeance; and all the time there was never the merest fractional excess over the '100'. It was truly a 'copybook' piece of running. In recent years I have travelled on these same locomotives when they were running considerably faster still, as I shall tell in the concluding chapter of this book. They are designed for a maximum speed of 135 m.p.h., and such is the tractive power built into them that an equally rapid run would have been made with the Mistral if the load had been sixteen and not fourteen coaches.

# 12 Southern Hemisphere

On one of my walls there is an attractively coloured certificate that reads:

KNOW ALL MEN THAT
Oswald Stevens Nock
while emplaned in a BOAC jetliner on
16 September 1968

did join that select band of travellers who have looked at one time on both the Northern and the Southern hemispheres by

CROSSING THE LINE
OF THE EQUATOR

It does not take long to get there nowadays. It was Sunday afternoon. We had finished tea on the terrace of our home in Bath, and were enjoying the late afternoon sunshine, when one of our neighbours called in to return a book she had borrowed, and we sat talking for half an hour or so. Then a Westinghouse staff car drove in through the gate, and I got up saying 'You'll have to excuse me, I must go now.' In response to her unspoken query I added 'I have an appointment with the Chief Engineer of the East African Railways at ten tomorrow morning, in Nairobi.' We laughed and I took my farewell of her and my wife.

A busy and varied three weeks lay ahead of me. Much of it promised, and indeed proved, to be hard work; and, apart from the pleasure of meeting business friends of long standing on their home ground, it was not very different from work at home. But my very first assignment, that in Kenya, was a delight. There were some points in a new signalling contract to be sorted out, and this involved a short tour 'out the line' in Equatorial Africa. With two signal engineers and one civil engineer as companions, and a native driver, we set out from Nairobi early one morning in a little petrol-driven 'buggy' to see the line as far west as the Great Rift Valley and inspect operating conditions at intermediate stations. It was the first time I had ever been in Africa, and on a beautiful morning I was enthralled as much by the countryside and the atmosphere as by the details of the railway working, which were being explained to me in great lucidity by my friends in the 'buggy'. Nairobi is at a high altitude above sea level, and it was not unduly hot, even though we were only just south of the Equator.

The railway is of course single-tracked throughout. In history it is one of the great romantic railways of the world, though not many of those involved in its construction, some 75 years ago would probably have felt there was much romance about it. In modern operating parlance the Uganda Railway, as it was known originally, was becoming saturated, and many considerations were being given to means of increasing its traffic carrying capacity. It was another instance of the kind of problem that had led to the production of the ECAFE book on single line railways, and an analysis of the train working at passing loops had led the EAR to the realization that much time was being spent at passing loops exchanging the tokens giving drivers authority to proceed into the next section. The technique of tokenless block working had greatly interested the EAR, and certain orders for equipment had been placed. But then there were local difficulties, and at one of the stations west of Nairobi my friends in the 'buggy' gave me a vivid illustration.

It was a country station out in the bush. It was difficult for me to detach myself from the sheer fascination of the African scene and get down to the brass tacks of train operation! An eastbound passenger train was expected and a positive swarm of native passengers, clad in all the colours of the rainbow, was sitting, lying, or lounging all over the station platform. Two westbound freight trains, both steam-hauled, were lying abreast of each other in sidings on the far side, and our little 'buggy'—an 'express passenger train'—was standing on the loop road. With one of the signal engineers I walked over to the stationmaster's office. He said that as the eastbound passenger train was on the line none of us could of course be given authority to proceed westwards; but once it arrived, and the block apparatus was freed, a token for the westbound direction could be issued. It would be given to the train with the highest priority. But then he added 'What is to be done when we have tokenless working? Which of those three trains is to go?' If the stationmaster had to walk across and speak to the driver all the time-saving of tokenless working would be lost. We agreed that signals were needed at the exit from each siding, to provide visual authority to proceed.

We drove on, ahead of the two freight trains, and, eventually coming to the summit of this part of the line, drew out on to the edge of the escarpment overlooking the Great Rift Valley. It was a tremendous prospect, with the vast extinct volcanic cone of Mount Longonot lying some fifty miles ahead on the far side of the valley.

We stopped at several other country stations to see the equipment and the working, and eventually arrived at the floor of the valley. In contrast to the lush, fertile land up in the hills, the ground had a dark, dead-looking appearance, and I was told it was the result of centuries of deposition of volcanic ash. Naivasha marked the limit of our westward inspection, and here we made a break for lunch, and a short trip by motorboat on the nearby lake. The ground is still unstable in this area, and small islands appear and disappear from time to time, and in places there were groups of dead trees, where the water had risen markedly. But no instability of the bottom could detract from the charm of Lake Naivasha, from the delicate foliage along its shores, or the exquisite colouring of masses of water lilies in some of the little bays. But this is a book about railways, not wild nature, and our cruising on the lake was brought to an end by the rapid approach of a violent thunderstorm.

Our return to Nairobi that afternoon was a time for my friends to tell many tales of the line, of encounters with wild animals, some of which had undoubtedly improved in the telling. But there was nothing apocryphal about the grisly relic I was shown on Nairobi station. This was the little four-wheeled saloon from which an early engineer of the line was dragged and killed by a man-eating lion.

There are some parts of the world where the dreams, indeed the wholly practical concepts, of famous men have gone awry, and of this there is no more poignant example than the Cape to Cairo Railway project, propounded and carried a long way towards realization by the vision of Cecil Rhodes. With the benefit of much hindsight one could write a great deal, nostalgically or cynically, about the way the ideals of that great Imperialist have not been realized; but for my own part I never fail to get a tremendous thrill from travelling over sections of what would have been the Cape to Cairo line, especially on the stretch, in his own Rhodesia, that goes north-westwards from Bulawayo to the Victoria Falls. Since my first visit to Southern Africa I have been over this line several times, as passenger, on the footplate of Beyer-Garratt locomotives on both passenger and freight trains, and on an inspection trolley. For most of the way there is nothing very distinctive about the scenery, indeed for a long way out of Bulawayo the line runs through low nondescript scrub, and it is not until near Dett that one comes into country where big game is to be seen.

The first station at which there is much more than a mere passing loop is Nyamandhlovu, where there are facilities for watering locomotives. A good try at the pronunciation is Yamanslova, and on one of my earliest trips I was told it meant 'meet of elephants'. I took it this referred to some neighbouring waterhole in this arid countryside, and quoted the translation in one of my articles. This brought an amusing letter from a man who had lived in Rhodesia, explaining that I had got the wrong kind of *meat*. It was apparently a place where, to please the whim of one of the old tribal chieftains, there had been a tremendous round-up and slaughter of elephants, and the natives had not gone short of meat for a long time afterwards. Where the line runs beside the great Wankie game reserve collisions with elephants are not infrequent, and against a Beyer-Garratt even the biggest of the 'jumbos' does not stand much chance. Then the natives swoop on to the carcase to replenish their larders. On one trip when my wife and I were enjoying the privilege of a trolley trip we stopped at Sawmills, an intermediate station in a wooded valley, where there is a signalling control panel for the colour-light signals and electric points installed throughout this route. But Sawmills is quite a little railway community, out in the bush; the men are engaged on track and signal maintenance, and in the little 'civic centre'—nothing more than a glorified hutment—their wives had laid on very attractive 'elevenses' for us. One could certainly appreciate the isolation in which railway staff and their families live on routes like this.

Not far beyond Sawmills the railway enters the longest length of straight track in Africa, the 72 miles from Gwaai to Dett. In the daytime, with the bush on either side, and frequently looking out for game, one does not notice this straightness particularly, but I was very conscious of it one night when I was travelling by the mail from the Victoria Falls to Bulawayo. At Sawmills, which we should reach just before dawn, I was due to go on to the footplate, and although there was a very reliable 'boy' to call me, I awoke soon after we left Dett, and lay in my berth looking up at a very starry sky. For what must have been nearly an hour the positions of the stars hardly changed. It was only when they did begin to move, that I realized we had reached the end of the long straight, and that we were not far from Sawmills. It was on this same train, some years earlier when I was riding on the footplate of one of the huge Beyer-Garratt locomotives, that I had my only sight of one of the 'big cats' from a train. It was a brilliant moonlit night and we were running through the thick bush country between the Victoria Falls and Thomson Junction. We were slowing down to stop at one of the intermediate stations and came round a curve in the line; there, drinking at the foot of the locomotive water column, was one of them. The driver thought it was a lioness, but directly she was caught in our headlight she made off smartly, and we could not be sure.

The bridge at the Victoria Falls, now a rather touchy frontier point between Rhodesia and Zambia, is one of the railway wonders of the world. It owes its remarkable location entirely to Cecil Rhodes, though strangely enough he never visited the Falls, and the bridge itself was not completed until after his death. But he was enthralled by descriptions of the tremendous spectacle, and the way in which the spray rose in a cloud at all times. He decreed that the railway should be carried near enough to the Falls for the carriages of passing trains to be wetted by the spray. No passenger trains now cross the bridge, though there is a certain interchange of freight. We went out almost to the centre of the bridge on a motor trolley. The international frontier is marked by a white line, and appropriately guarded. It was a stirring sight to see one of the enormous '20' class 4–8–2 + 2–8–4 Garratts bringing a train of about 2,000 tons over this great bridge.

One of my most amusing memories of days 'out the line' in Rhodesia was on a day when I went to make an inspection of the signal control panel at Gwelo, on the Bulawayo–Salisbury main line. I was taken there by a fast car but my railway friends, knowing my appetite for punishment where steam locomotives are concerned, arranged for me to ride back part of the way on the engine of a freight train. This was no late evening or moonlight jaunt. It was high noon, with the thermometer well into the nineties. I thought of Sir Noel Coward. 'Mad dogs and Englishmen' indeed! But any thoughts of discomfort were banished when I climbed up to the footplate of a '19D' 4–8–2, amid all the familiar smells. The line was busy. At three successive loops we passed heavy freight trains, and it was interesting also to see how well the colour-light signals showed up, miles ahead, in the shimmering noonday heat. My host was waiting with the car at Shangani, but equally welcome was the sight of a pleasant little pub adjoining the station. Need I say more, after a grilling two hours on the footplate!

The 'howling wilderness' of De Aar—so Lennox van Onselen described the site of what is now one of the most important railway junctions in the Southern Hemisphere. De Aar is certainly an out-and-out railway settlement, in the midst of the high veldt in the north of Cape Province. It is a very major crossroads of trunk lines, running north to the great cities of the Transvaal, and to the 'Cape to Cairo' line, south-east to Port Elizabeth, north-west to Windhoek, and south to the Cape itself. But its fascination for me was as a locomotive centre, remarkable in that none but the hugest of South African steam found employment there. Even at the largest and most modern depot one can usually find a few old-timers doing shunting and pilot duties, and in South Africa itself, when I made a round tour in 1968, I found plenty of them in the big sheds on the Reef, at Bloemfontein, Kimberley, Port Elizabeth and Cape Town; but there was nothing like that about De Aar. I could quite imagine it can be a bleak and unhospitable place in winter storms, when the winds drive the dust from months of cold rainless weather into every crevice; but the day when we paused there for an afternoon on our way to the Cape was blessed with serene cloudless sunshine, and out in the locomotive yard I watched and photographed to my heart's content.

De Aar was then the spiritual home of the greatest of all South African non-articulated steam locomotives, the great '25' class 4–8–4s. Standing beside them it is difficult to believe that they run on no wider than the 3 ft 6 in. gauge, and yet they are taller, heavier and wider than anything that has ever run in Great Britain. Their job was not only the haulage of very heavy trains; it had got to be done across a largely waterless desert country. Ninety out of the 140 for which the South African Railways placed contracts in 1951 had special tenders with condensing apparatus, so that the same water could be used over and over again. The engines themselves are large enough in all conscience, having an overall length of 49 ft 7 in.; but the condensing tenders are much longer, having a length of 60 ft 5 in. At De Aar I saw these extraordinary locomotives coming and going. Some of the freight trains were of such length as to require *two* of them, while on the shed, and participating in the heavy traffic, were the slightly smaller '23' class 4–8–2s. One of these giants was doing pilot work, and this included the spectacular job of pushing a train of loaded coal wagons up on to the high gallery, where they are emptied into bunkers, for loading up the tenders of the road locomotives. At some other sheds the veterans were in use for this humping duty; but to see a '23' retreating some distance, taking a tearing run at the steep incline up the loading gallery, and finishing on the high stage some 46 feet almost vertically above us, was awe-inspiring to the last degree.

I now cross to the land of 'down under' in the reverse direction to which my wife and I have several times made the journey. Flying 'with the sun' can be disconcerting at times, and not too kind to the digestion, when the modern jetliners allow you to lunch in Perth, Western Australia, and your hosts in South Africa have a dinner party laid on to greet you in Johannesburg, after you have been flying for about twelve hours and been fed liberally on the way!

We went to Australia first in 1969, in my year of office as President of the Institution of Railway Signal Engineers, and in travels that took us to all the state capitals except Hobart we used the night expresses for most of the long journeys. Riding in the luxury of sleeping cars is not quite the same as being 'out the line'. But while we were in New South Wales a 'combined operation' for members of the Institution and their ladies was organized in the Newcastle district. Transport was being arranged by a fleet of private cars, but the existence of my other 'hats' was not unknown in Australia, and it was hinted that if I cared to travel instead by the morning 'Newcastle Flyer' from Sydney I should be there in plenty of time to join the official party and preside at the lunch that was laid on. It was added that footplate passes could be arranged. Could a duck swim! Con Cardew, lately retired from being Assistant Chief Mechanical Engineer of the New South Wales Railways, with whom I had corresponded previously, would come with me. And so, while Harold Bourne, the Chief Signal Engineer, and his wife took my wife, and gave her a wonderful sightseeing run, I went down to the Central Station and collected an old overall 'slop', in case we had steam haulage on the second half of the journey.

Even when I met Con Cardew on the platform it was not known whether we should have steam or diesel from Gosford onwards; but I was interested to find that the enginemen on the smart electric locomotive that was to run the first half of the journey would be continuing through to Newcastle, taking whatever form of motive power was provided from Gosford. It proved a fascinating run. Cardew, who sadly died two years ago, was one of those able and enthusiastic souls who had steam in his very veins. He had a distinguished career, all in New South Wales, was a pillar of the Australian section of the Institution of Locomotive Engineers, and in his retirement was keen enough to come out on the footplate and delight in escorting his visitor. The electric part of the journey was absorbing in the insight it gave me into the teeming railway activity of the Sydney suburban area, and then in the climb southwards to the hills overlooking the Hawkesbury river, where I saw within days of our first arrival in Australia some of the most beautiful scenery the land has to offer.

The railway makes a precipitous descent, much of it on a gradient of 1 in 40, which puts one in mind of the Lötschberg or the Bhor Ghat. But there is no other similarity, for our driver, easing us down the gradient, was bringing us into sight of a complex of estuaries like a vastly extended and deeper version of the river Fal, in Cornwall, with its numerous creeks and densely wooded inlets leading out into the main stream. The Hawkesbury river has all the same sylvan beauty, but with much higher flanking hills, and oyster beds along some of the shores. I was entranced, and delighted that the slow speed at which we came down the gradient and crossed the great ten-span girder bridge across the main channel enabled me to drink in the sublime beauty of the scene without having to divide my attention between nature and the locomotive working. Once across the main stream we began to make faster time, and through one of the many rocky eminences we threaded the Woy Woy Tunnel, the longest in Australia, just over a mile long and quite straight. So, after a run of 29¼ miles from Hornsby, in the outer suburbs of Sydney, made in 40½ minutes, we came to Gosford, and the end of the electrified part of the line. To Cardew's delight, and to mine no less, a steam 'Pacific' of the massive 'C38' class was waiting to take us forward.

Con himself took the regulator; the driver who had handled the electric locomotive so expertly from Sydney became the fireman, and the 'second man' had the unexpected leisure of a ride 'on the cushions' to Newcastle. The 'C38' is a big, robustly-built workhorse of a locomotive. There are no frills, no undue refinements of design, other than those that provide long mileages between visits to works for overhaul and completely trouble-free service on the road. Con Cardew drove her good and hard, and over on the right-hand side of the footplate I was conscious of a machine very much akin to the 'Black Five' 4–6–0s of the LMS, and the '15 F' 4–8–2s of the South African Railways. The engine rode hard but quite steadily at speeds up to 70 m.p.h. on an undulating track through typical Australian bush country. There was no lack of steep gradients, and indeed we went hammering up a short gradient of 1 in 44 from Dora's Creek. We ran the 38¼ miles from Gosford to Fassifern in 43¾ minutes, start to stop, but of that distance 31¾ miles had been run in no more than 33¾ minutes. It was an exhilarating spin. I did not go right into Newcastle, because my signalling friends had arranged to meet me at Fassifern and take me by car to the luncheon rendezvous with the rest of the party. There was just time to wash my face (and neck!) and then quickly to assume my other hat for the rest of the day.

One of the most unusual journeys I had in Australia was that across the Nullarbor Plain, by the Trans-Australian express, which ran from Port Pirie, South Australia, to Perth. This was before the standard-gauge line from Broken Hill, New South Wales, to Port Pirie was completed and the world famous Indian Pacific began to run through from Sydney to Perth. No country has been more bedevilled by changes of rail gauge than Australia, and when my wife and I were travelling west from Adelaide, we had to change from the 5 ft 3 in. gauge train to the standard-gauge Trans-Australian at Port Pirie. This was a luxury sleeping car express on which we lived for the best part of two days, and for me the highlight of a very long journey was the spell I was able to spend in the locomotive cab while we were crossing the Nullarbor Plain. I have already referred in this book to certain lengthy stretches of straight track, such as the one across the Rhone delta between Marseilles and Arles, on the former PLM line, and that between Gwaai and Dett on the 'Cape to Cairo' route; but all these fade into complete insignificance beside this Australian phenomenon, because over the Nullarbor Plain the line is straight for 297 miles!

The name means 'no trees'; actually there is precious little of anything—just the low, thin, scrubby salt-bush in places, no birds, no water, no animals, no people. The 'stations' were created purely to provide bases for men concerned with the maintenance of the line, and at the staging points where one locomotive crew relieved another. It was an amazing experience to ride the diesel in such a terrain. The landscape seemed flat in all directions, and one could sense the curvature of the earth just as at sea—indeed, when we were approaching a station or crossing place, we saw the tops of the buildings first, just as one sights the masts and funnels of ships at sea, before the hull comes into view. Under a fierce sun, in a cloudless sky, we bowled along at 60 m.p.h. Back in the train life was rather like that of a ship, with passengers meeting regularly for meals, and foregathering afterwards to take coffee in the lounge car and listen while one of our number played the piano. We reached Perth soon after breakfast on the following morning.

If however one wishes to go really out into the wilds on Australian railways, the north-west of Western Australia is the place to go, where the Hamersley Iron Company has its own private railway to bring ore from its great mines at Mount Tom Price and Paraburdoo down to the coast at Dampier for shipment to Japan. The only practicable way to get to Dampier is to fly from Perth, and I shall never forget my first sight of the railway as our aircraft circled over the port before landing. The arid, red-looking country was spread out in limitless extent, and the richness of the colouring, enhanced by the dazzling white of the salt pans just inland, was that of minerals in the soil. Soon after landing I was taken to see the magnificent workshops at Mile 7. Planners talk of being able to start with a clean sheet. Here, apart from the red dust, there was absolutely nothing: a range of low hills to the south, a line of rocky hillocks that mark the coast to the north, and apart from this and the sight of an occasional car speeding along the road to the airport, nothing but the limitless expanse of red sandy flats.

The diesel-hauled trains bring the ore down fifteen *thousand* tons at a time, in 150-car trains. They were running five of these great trains a day when I was there in 1972, but since then the output has been intensified, with the opening of the spectacular extension of the line from Tom Price to Paraburdoo. The loaded run of 182 miles from Tom Price to Dampier was taking about six hours, too long unfortunately for me to have a ride on one of the trains. Time was not on my side, and I had to fly between the two centres of activity in a tiny five-seater monoplane. But I saw these great trains on the run, and to stand at the lineside in this rugged country, and to see and *feel* one of them go by at 40 m.p.h., is an experience not readily forgotten. The locomotives, which are worked in pairs, are each of 3,900 horsepower, but each of the 150 cars in the train weighs 120 tons loaded, 30 tons per axle. When one reflects that few British locomotives or freight vehicles have axle loads of more than 20 tons, the pounding on the rails as one of these juggernauts passes—six hundred axles in succession, each with a 30-ton load, to say nothing of the locomotives—it will be appreciated what I mean by the *feel* of a train as it passes!

# 13 Storm and Tempest

The story now goes back briefly to 1936, when the landscape of Strathspey was gripped deeply by the January frost. The sharp exhausts of the engines of the Mail had echoed back from the frozen cutting sides as we climbed with the Pass of Druimuacdhar, and then the beautiful sight of snow-clad mountains in the winter dawn had vanished as the clouds rolled up and Strathspey had greeted us with a blizzard. Soon we could see little or nothing of the line ahead; ice packed up against the cab glasses, and the drivers of our two engines were slowing down in order to get a definite sight of signals. Then quite suddenly we ran out of the storm and it was briefly clear when we arrived at Aviemore, and some remarshalling of the train took place and engines were changed. For the last stage of the run to Inverness we got a fresh 'Black Five' 4–6–0, with one of the veteran Highland 4–6–0s of 1902, the *Beaufort Castle*, to assist up the heavy ascent to the second major summit on the journey, in the pass of Slochd Muick, at 1,319 ft above sea level. There was every sign that the snow storms would soon be resumed, but the opportunity of riding on a member of such a famous vintage class was not to be resisted even though there was scant protection from the weather, compared to that on the big modern engine coupled next to the train.

When the *Beaufort Castle* was built the days were not so far distant when the enginemen had little more than a weatherboard in front of them; and on one railway when a kindly superintendent first put on a semblance of a cab the men thanked him for his solicitude, but said 'please take them off; we can't see'! On the *Beaufort Castle* a tarpaulin was stretched from the cab roof to the front of the tender to give some shelter. These men were assisting the Mail only up to Slochd. After coupling off, they would be returning to Aviemore tender-first, and that tarpaulin was more for the return journey than to give much more protection than the cab when running forwards. We were hardly underway before it was snowing again, but in the interest of watching the operation of this splendid old engine I hardly noticed that the icy wind from the north was driving snow clean through the cab. Veteran she might be, but she was giving no half-hearted assistance to the engine behind, and her steady, even, thunderous, beat was completely drowning the exhaust noise of the 'Black Five'. My frequent notes were smudged by snow lighting on my book; but this was 'out the line' in very truth, on the railway where the phrase originated.

Here I may interpose that the job of recording locomotive work on the footplate was an acquired art. The business of taking the times of passing intermediate stations, of clocking the speeds by stopwatch from the mileposts which was no more than occasionally hazardous in the train from the attention of fellow passengers, became altogether more tricky on a swaying or vibrating engine. There would be coal dust flying, spray from the hose blown on the wind, and at night the need to read one's watches in the glare of the fire—and all the time to keep out of the way of driver and fireman. But it was certainly a new experience to get smothered in snow into the bargain!

We stopped at Carr Bridge to cross the morning southbound passenger train from Inverness, and then started again up the heaviest part of the ascent. Blizzard conditions were now on us in earnest. Snow was driving level, clean through the cab, and it was only the heat of the fire that kept me from becoming completely white on my right-hand side. Blizzard or not, the two engines were soon fairly 'lifting' their heavy train of more than 400 tons, and the noise they made about it sounded to me as a symphony of robust human effort and engineering mastery over the job. The sound of a steam locomotive fighting hard up a gradient is music in the ears of all true railwaymen, and I can well believe the story of a little group of American 'hoggers', deadheading back to their home station, sitting up at night listening to a great engine working steam, when they might have lain down and slept. Had the weather been clear I should have seen we were mounting into wild, desolate country, on the flanks of the Monadhliath Mountains, but in this blinding snowstorm we could see nothing. It was only when we curved round rightwards and pounded through a narrow vertical-sided rock cutting that I knew we were nearing Slochd summit. I climbed down from the *Beaufort Castle* wet with the melted snow on my overalls, and my hands numb with the cold, but I would not have missed that part of the run for worlds. The downhill run of 22½ miles to Inverness would have been an anticlimax had I not gone forward on arrival and seen every cold part of our engine absolutely plastered with snow. On hearing what we had come through, the locomotive foreman who met us in said at once 'We shall have to get the ploughs out.' They did, and the trains continued running normally.

There is nothing the locomotive enginemen dreads more than fog.

In areas of semaphore signalling, when one is speeding along and all at once the obliterating blanket descends, there is always the fear that it may have come on so suddenly that the fog men are not yet out, and that one might not get the warning detonator at an adverse distant signal. Then if the warning 'bang' does come, there is the agonizing crawl up to the home signal, not knowing if it is on or off. We experienced all these sentiments when I was riding up from Leicester one afternoon in 1948 on the footplate of one of the then new 'B1' class 4–6–0s of the London and North Eastern Railway. It was a beautifully fine winter's day, inclined to frost, and as we neared Aylesbury the sun was setting in a cloudless sky. We drew in to make our last passenger stop, and another engineman returning to London joined us on the footplate rather than ride on the cushions. He brought the unwelcome news that it was very foggy ahead. I shall never forget the look on our driver's face. He certainly welcomed another experienced man at his elbow to help sight the signals. We started from Aylesbury well enough. On the steep rise towards the northern crest of the Chilterns, gradient 1 in 117, we climbed well, with speed rising to 34 m.p.h. by Stoke Mandeville; but by Wendover the mist was changing to a thick white fog. We could still see the semaphore signals however, and we topped the gradient with the engine steaming hard. But once we were over the crest and descending towards Great Missenden conditions soon began to deteriorate. All eyes were straining for a sight of the distant signal for that interlocking. It was 'right away', and we went on with confidence into a thick blanket of fog at 60 m.p.h.

Amersham showed us a clear 'distant' too, and we began the steep descent to Rickmansworth. Speed was creeping up to 60 again in the deep chalk cuttings near Chalfont, then 'bang!', we had exploded a detonator. Chorley Wood 'distant' was on, and speed was brought down to dead slow. We crawled forward into a fog that had noticeably thickened in the last few miles, so much so that when we did see the home signal at danger we very nearly overran it. The next half-hour was the most uncomfortable I ever remember on a locomotive. We were held for nearly four minutes at Chorley Wood, and then we went on slowly to receive another 'bang' as we approached Rickmansworth. The signals here were pulled off in time to avoid bringing us to a dead stand, and then we passed into the area of day colour-light signals. Such signals are generally considered to be much more helpful to a driver than semaphores, but everything in railway working needs qualification, as I was to experience now in full measure.

By this time the fog had developed into a real old-fashioned 'pea-souper', thick and yellow and dark overhead. At once we missed the friendly bangs of the detonators to warn us when the 'distants' were on, for in the colour-light area no fogmen are employed. Those closely-spaced signals are all equipped with automatic train stops, but these, while admirable in safeguarding an intense electric train service, were no comfort to us, because our engine was not fitted with the trip gear for applying the brake if we should overrun a danger signal. We had to grope our way at 10 to 15 m.p.h. from one signal to the next through fog so dense that the powerful beams of the colour lights could not be seen until we were about 15 yards from each post. In any case such conditions would call for extreme vigilance, but from the number of 'yellows' we were getting it was evident that another train was only just ahead. In this way it took us 24 minutes to cover the 8 miles from Rickmansworth to Harrow. Through Harrow it was so thick that the fireman and I, looking for the starting signal, here on the right-hand side, did not see it showing green until the front of the engine was just level with the post!

Fortunately now however we were passing from the old Joint Line, shared with the Metropolitan, on to a stretch that was once purely Great Central, equipped with semaphore signals, and with the fogmen at their posts. We began to run much more briskly now, passing abreast of the Metropolitan station at Wembley Park at 50 m.p.h., but approaching Neasden North it was so dark and thick that we missed the distant signal altogether. There was no 'bang', but not having seen the signal at all we could take no chances; brakes on, and a crawl up towards the signal box. The signalman must have guessed our uncertainty, for he threw open the window and shouted across 'You're all right; you're right away.' Then strangely enough the fog was not on the ground in the inner suburbs. It was black as night overhead, but the colour-light signals from Neasden inwards showed up clearly, and we were able to run at about 50 m.p.h. to the entrance to the long tunnel that leads down into Marylebone goods yard. But the finish was positively traumatic. The yard itself was dense and pitch dark, and when we finally crept into the terminus we might have been in the open country for all we could see of its walls and roof, and at the platform end a man was waving a brazier to show us where the buffer stops were! With all the anti-pollution methods now being applied fogs like that are now little more than a memory; but for me it was another experience that I would not have missed.

Another experience, to the excitement of which fog contributed, came in late November 1958 on the high-speed Bristolian express, then booked to run the 118½ miles from Paddington to Bristol non-stop in 105 minutes. I had ridden several times on the footplate of locomotives working this fine service, but I was anxious to obtain some data from one of the 'Castle' class engines recently fitted with twin-orifice blastpipes and double chimneys. They had the reputation of being very free running, and I was hoping to notch up a 'ton', descending the Dauntsey Bank. I had done it once before with a 'King' class engine, when I was travelling passenger, but not yet when I was on the footplate. The particular engine on this November morning, the *Bristol Castle*, had something of a history, which is worth retelling once again. In 1952, after the death of His Majesty King George VI, the Western Region wished to use the engine *Windsor Castle* for the Royal funeral train. During a state visit to Swindon in 1924 it had been driven by the late King's father, and bore a plaque commemorating the event. It had also been used for his funeral train, in 1936. But in 1952 the engine *Windsor Castle*, No. 4082, had amassed a high mileage since last general overhaul and was not considered in good enough condition to take such an important duty. So the name and number plates were exchanged with a recent member of the class, built new in 1948, the *Bristol Castle*, together with the commemorative plaques.

One look at the engine hauling the Royal funeral train from Paddington to Windsor in February 1952 was enough to show a connoisseur of Great Western locomotives that it could not possibly be the real *Windsor Castle*. Certain details of design marked it definitely as one of the post-war batch. British Railways were accused of deception, and had eventually to 'come clean'. The commemorative plaques were discreetly removed, but the engine that had been outshopped as No. 7013 *Bristol Castle*, remained No. 4082 *Windsor Castle* to the end of its working life. And here was I, in November 1958, about to ride the real *Windsor Castle*, but under her assumed trappings as No. 7013 *Bristol Castle*. The chassis and many of the fittings were then 34 years old, though of course the boiler, and parts such as cylinders and valves, had been replaced—the boiler several times. As regards the changeover of names a wag once referred to her as the 'Jekyll and Hyde' engine! It was rather misty in London that morning but, on the former Great Western main lines, no one had any apprehensions about fog, with the automatic train control apparatus and its distinctive audible signals in the engine cab.

We went out of London as confidently as on the most serene summer day, topping 70 m.p.h. soon after Ealing, and running at 76–7 m.p.h. until a slight easing to 60 m.p.h. was needed over a piece of track temporarily not up to the highest standards. All signals were clear at first, and on the approach to each 'distant' signal we received a loud ring on the bell in the cab. We quickly resumed 75 m.p.h. after Slough, with the weather really thick but white after

Maidenhead. We were approaching Reading at 76 m.p.h. when the warning siren went: a distant signal 'on', and we had to stop at Reading East. For the next ten miles or so things were somewhat disorganized. On the main road crossing over the railway to the west of Pangbourne, the driver of a lorry had misjudged his distance in the fog and crashed into the parapet of the bridge. We were stopped again, and warned to go cautiously, and finally, again, a third time, at the bridge itself, to assure ourselves there was no debris on the line. By the time we were doing 70 m.p.h. again, at Cholsey, we had spent nearly 27 minutes over the preceding 15 miles, and we passed Didcot a quarter of an hour later.

Although the weather was clearing somewhat by that time and we had a clear road, there was no point in pressing things unduly. The most we might have recovered with a truly all-out effort would have been 3 or 4 minutes, and so from Didcot onwards up the long, slight rise through the Vale of the White Horse we ran at 71 to 73 m.p.h., and interest now became centred upon what we might do down the Dauntsey Bank. It was no occasion for going for a record. I was more interested to see how the engine would accelerate under normal steaming conditions. We came to the crest of that two-mile descent at 1 in 100 doing 82 m.p.h.; by the foot of the gradient we had shot up to 95 m.p.h., but that was all, and on the gentle rise that followed speed tailed off to 72 m.p.h. when we entered Box Tunnel. But after the hazards earlier in the journey it had been pleasant to be able to run the 56 miles from Cholsey to Bathampton in a shade under 45 minutes—exactly 75 m.p.h. average. With another check for permanent way work west of Bath we were eventually 14 minutes late in reaching Bristol, but even so making an average speed of all but 60 m.p.h. from Paddington, all checks included.

My next tale of hazards on the line takes us to the South of France. In Chapter 11 of this book I have written of the immaculate high speed performance of *Le Mistral* between Paris and Dijon. The later stages of that journey were more eventful than the beginning. We continued to make very fast time between Dijon and Lyons, but when we got away on the next stage, to Valence, the weather had become very stormy. I was no longer in the driver's cab, but I could see from the train the country ahead was in the throes of very violent thunderstorms. We were soon in the thick of it, with torrential rain and a wind that was bending tall trees like saplings, and we did well in the circumstances to cover that 66 miles to Valence in 54 minutes. But on getting away again we soon came to a stand in open country. Lightning had struck one of the railway power supply substations and there was no current on the overhead line. And there we sat, for nearly an hour, while the curtain of rain was so intense that at times

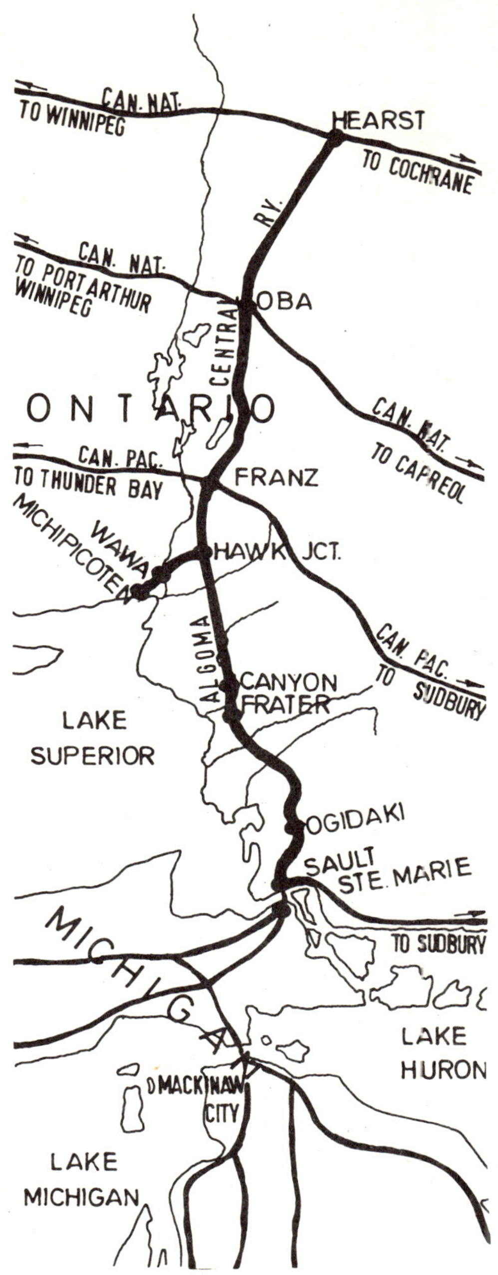


Fig. 5 The Algoma Central Railway

we could hardly see through the window, and only the largest vehicles were continuing to run on the nearby highway—so furious was the cross-wind.

Rather than chafe at the delay, I thought instead of the *cheminots* who, in such appalling weather conditions, would be working might and main to get the power supply restored; and that we were under way again in less than an hour speaks volumes for their efforts. We arrived in Avignon 72 minutes late, having taken just over two hours to cover the $77\frac{1}{4}$ miles from Valence. It was still very stormy in the Rhone delta, though on this wild evening it was not the traditional mistral that was blowing. Fortunately full power was available on the line to the south, and we stormed over the remaining $75\frac{1}{4}$ miles to Marseilles in $54\frac{3}{4}$ minutes, reaching a full 100 m.p.h. several times. But it was a strange beginning to a fortnight of glorious holiday weather on the Côte d'Azur!

Throughout the month of April 1974 I was in West Ontario, working on the Algoma Central Railway. Although it is one of the smallest of Canadian railways, it is one of the most fascinating, in its chequered history and in the magnificent scenery through which it runs. When I was asked to write a book about it, arrangements were made for me to go to Sault Ste Marie at the end of the summer, in 1973, when the autumn colouring in the forests would be at its finest, and ice had not begun to close the Great Lakes to shipping. This is a railway of diverse activity, and the book I was commissioned to write was to cover it all. But a serious, though happily transient, illness involving surgery prevented my going as originally planned, and I went early in the following spring when waterborne traffic was just restarting on the Great Lakes. It was still very cold when I reached 'the Soo', as Sault Ste Marie is universally known, with freshly fallen snow lying in the country around; and I hoped that when the time came to go 'out the line' I should see the rugged country to the north in some remnants of its winter garb.

In the first week I was there I was invited to join an inspection trip covering the whole length of the main line: 300 miles north to a junction with the former National Transcontinental line—now part of the Canadian National—at Hearst. We should be four days away, and my companions would be Russ Rankin, the General Superintendent, Don Burns, Chief Engineer, and Hugh Paul, the Traffic Manager. Before I begin our journey, however, the vehicle in which we were to live for those four days merits more than just a passing mention. In North America these officers' saloons are known as 'business cars', and this one, the *Michipicoten*, was an enormously heavy twelve-wheeler formerly owned by the New York Central, and weighing no less than 94 tons. When one recalls that a modern

British passenger coach weighs about 33 tons it will be appreciated what an affair the *Michipicoten* is. It contains four sleeping berths for officers, a dining room and an observation lounge, and our welfare was provided for by a steward who combined the functions of cook, housemaid, and being ready to participate in purely railway tasks like helping the brakemen, when coupling up and so on. Our man, Stan Chapman, was a treasure. The business car was to be attached to trains as required, passenger and freight alike.

On the first day we set out from the Soo coupled just behind the four diesel-electric locomotives of a heavy northbound freight train; we had 63 cars and a caboose behind us, though as many of these cars were returning empties the total tonnage of 1,800 was considered light by Algoma Central Railway standards. All the locomotives were of what is sometimes described as the 'second generation' of diesels, on which, except for the cab, the casing is made no wider than necessary to cover the machinery, with external walkways on either side. It was along these walkways, four in succession, that Russ Rankin took me, once we were under way, to reach the driver's cab of the leading locomotive. I soon realized I was not too late in the season to see the winter wonderland of Algoma. Snow was lying deeply. The many lakes were completely frozen over, with a thickness of about a foot and a half of solid ice, and covered deeply in snow, while on the sides of rock cuttings many waterfalls had been frozen solid, and in their vivid green and white colouring presented a remarkable effect. The line is of course single-tracked throughout, and when at passing loops we met southbound freight trains I realized why the Algoma people regarded our train as a 'light' one. These southbound trains had each got more than *five thousand* tons. With a number of stops on the way, and much heavy slogging at about 20 m.p.h. up steep gradients, it was evening when we reached Hawk Junction, 165 miles to the north. There the business car was detached and parked in a siding for the night.

Hawk Junction is the most important intermediate point on the line for purely Algoma traffic. From it the branch line bears away to the west towards the great iron mining centre of Wawa, where most of the heavy mineral traffic of the line originates. It continues to Michipicoten Harbour, on Lake Superior, but at that time of year the whole place was completely iced up. During the evening several of the local railwaymen called in, including Newall Mills, the dynamic trainmaster. We all turned in early for there was another long day ahead of us, culminating in a social gathering at Hearst. But I do not think any of us, even the local men, anticipated the kind of weather the next morning would bring. When I say that we awoke to a blizzard, that must be an understatement—at any rate in relation to my North Country English experience. Russ Rankin called me to see a freight train arriving from the south. Its locomotives were absolutely plastered with snow, while outside there were no snowflakes as such; a fine thick white dust was just driving level. Except where a locomotive had just moved, no rails were visible at all, and standing cars in the sidings were already snowed up above their axles.

We were going north on a 4,000-ton freight ordered out before eleven o'clock but, as there is something of a gradient for the first five miles out of Hawk Junction, Newall Mills organised a snow plough to go up ahead of us and clear the tracks. To make sure of things *four* diesel locomotives were put behind that snow plough. Apart from the immediate start the gradients are not difficult north of Hawk Junction and, even though our two diesels had 4,000 tons behind them, we would do our own ploughing. Well wrapped up against the weather, I climbed from the business car along the outside of those two diesels and was welcomed by Engineer Kuyec on the leader. By any British or West European standards the conditions were appalling; but Canadian railways are geared to winter conditions, and Kuyec, his co-driver and the front brakeman enjoyed having a visitor to whom they could show their craft. Even where the snow plough had been less than an hour earlier, the rails were barely visible, while alongside the line the forests of firs were bowed down by the weight of snow. Some were newly broken. The windscreen wipers could barely keep the lookout clear, not that we could see very far anyway through that whirlwind of fine snow. Although it was single track and the visibility was so limited, there was consolation in knowing we had the line to ourselves. The only other train was the daily 'passenger' from the Soo, and as yet she was far behind us.

Just beyond the top of that initial gradient we came to Alden, the crossing station that had been the limit of the snow plough patrol from Hawk Junction. We could see clearly how far they had been, for ahead on the ploughed but now almost concealed track was a pile of snow, and beyond it just limitless white. We were travelling at 27 m.p.h. when the small plough on the front of our own locomotive hit that heap. Instantly we were smothered. Moreover that first avalanche was not all. The snow was being flung up faster than the screen wipers could clear it, and at times we were running literally blind. In the cab it was dark, for the side windows were being choked with the driving snow; yet on we went, with speed sometimes rising to nearly 40 m.p.h. The back doors of the cab were almost obscured, but through what was left of the lookout it was amazing to see the leading cars of that great train winding round the curves behind us, becoming gradually plastered with snow all over their sides and roofs.

Suddenly the alarm bell began to ring in the cab. The engines were overheating! This might seem astonishing in such weather, but Kuyec and his colleagues guessed at once what was the matter, and we stopped. The snow on the sides of the locomotives had packed up over the ventilation grilles, and no cooling air could get in. The co-driver and the front brakeman prepared for action; but the first thing was to get out of that cab. Snow had packed in so tightly on the *back* side that at first the door could not be opened. But hefty bucking by two big chaps managed to wedge it far enough to get a shovel through the narrow opening, and then they began to dig. They had to shovel their way along the outside platform, on which there was about two feet of snow; scrape the snow off the sides and free the air intakes, and then do the same on the second locomotive. That we were under way again in no more than 25 minutes is a testimony to the energy with which those two stalwarts set about the job.

Our next stop was at Franz, where the Algoma Central intersects the main line of the Canadian Pacific, and climbing back along our two locomotives and seeing them from the business car I was still more astonished; for we had *two feet* of snow piled up on top of our locomotives. The photographs I took while they were shunting some cars into the Canadian Pacific sidings speak more than pages of description. Other cars waiting to be taken by the next westbound freight train were snowed up level with their running boards. The thing that impressed me more than anything else, however, was that, although my friends in the business car agreed that conditions were severe, and rather exceptional for April, there was never a moment's thought of carrying on other than normally. The only concession made was before we left Hawk Junction that morning, when Rankin agreed to a slight reduction in the load of one of the southbound freights. Mills was apprehensive that they might be in trouble on the heavy gradients to the south and the load was therefore reduced from 5,600 to 5,000 tons; but that was all! Although it remained very cold the snow eased after we left Franz, and we reached Hearst under clear skies; and as if to mock our struggles of the previous day our return, attached to next morning's passenger train, was in cloudless sunshine and amid visions of the snowbound countryside that left me speechless with wonder at times.

# 14 In the Steps of Van Horne

When we were doing our shunting at Franz on that bleak April day in 1974, with short lines of freight cars standing forlorn in the snow and the picturesque water tower of steam days looking like some medieval turret in an ice-bound landscape in south-eastern Europe, one might have found it hard to believe that the single-tracked line intersecting that of the Algoma Central, with its tiny station building, was one of the greatest lifelines of North America, the railway that His Majesty King George V once called 'the steel of Empire'. The inception and building of the Canadian Pacific Railway was indeed a symbol of the nineteenth-century development of the British Empire, and behind it all loomed the gigantic personality of William Cornelius Van Horne. It might perhaps be invidious to suggest that this mighty American-born entrepreneur, knighted and decorated by Queen Victoria, was the greatest all-round railwayman who has ever lived; but his talents were so diverse, his achievements in so many facets of railway activity so far-reaching, as to go far to substantiate such an assertion.

One could say that he had the pioneer vision of Cecil Rhodes, the wiles of a Mark Huish, the contractor's tenacity of 'Georgie Porgie' Pauling, the operating skill of Cecil Paget, and the sagacity in management of Richard Moon, or Ralph Wedgwood. And if necessary he could quite well have managed the locomotive department too, because in early days on the CPR he frequently drove the engine of his own train. My friend Omer Lavallee of Montreal has written a book about the Canadian Pacific which he has entitled *Van Horne's Road*; and the extent to which the aura, success and influence of the CPR extends over Canada certainly suggested to me that when I was 'out the line' anywhere in the Dominion I was walking, riding, or indeed flying in the steps of Van Horne. Yes, one can also fly today, very swiftly and comfortably too, by Canadian Pacific.

I shall never forget my first sight of a Canadian train. It was very fittingly at Windsor station, Montreal, a terminus of CP Rail. I had, barely an hour earlier, arrived in Canada having flown the Atlantic.

Omer Lavallee and another Canadian, Ed Jordan, who has since become a close family friend, were quite determined that I should see something of Canadian railways before they entertained me to a gargantuan meal; and we went to Windsor station. There I saw and gasped at one of the double-decker commuter trains. The sheer height of it staggered me! I shall never forget when O. V. S. Bulleid, the ingenious, but somewhat eccentric assistant to Sir Nigel Gresley who became Chief Mechanical Engineer of the Southern, tried to alleviate the overcrowding situation on the Eastern Section suburban trains and built some double-decker coaches. With overall height limited to 13 ft above rail level not only was the headroom much limited and giving a somewhat claustrophobic effect, but it took a long time to load and unload. How Bulleid would have welcomed the chance to build coaches *eighteen feet* high! Perhaps he might have been tempted to try triple-deckers.

These enormous CP Rail coaches were among the first I travelled in on the Canadian railways. I was taken out for a relatively short ride at midday, to Hudson, a charming residential area on the south side of the Lac des Deux Montagnes. These trains work on the push and pull principle. The enormous double-decker coaches are hauled on the outward journey by a diesel-electric locomotive; but at the terminal point the locomotive remains *in situ*, and on the return is remotely controlled from the driver's cab in the leading coach of the train. I rode with the driver in both directions, but it was of course the return run, at such a tremendous height above rail level, that was the more interesting. The riding, at such a height, was very good, seeing that any slight rolling that would hardly be noticeable on the bottom deck would naturally be accentuated 'upstairs'.

In setting out to travel right across Canada by train I began on a somewhat zigzag course, going south-west to Toronto, then by the Ontario Northland Railway up to Arctic tidewaters at Moosonee, on Hudson Bay, and south by road coach to North Bay, where late at night I joined the great transcontinental luxury train of CP Rail, The Canadian, en route for Winnipeg. The steward called me next morning in time for me to go forward to ride the leading diesel from White River westwards. Railway divisional point it may be, but the place itself is little more than a settlement, deep in the woods. It was a misty morning, with the straight-stemmed firs dripping and motionless in the still air. Apart from our two diesels and the fine stainless steel carriages, it could have looked much the same as when Van Horne's 'army' hacked their way through just over ninety years ago. The American tycoon who introduced Van Horne to the Canadian Pacific, the one-eyed Jim Hill, fought tooth and nail to get the line routed through Sault Ste Marie and the south side of Lake Superior.

That would have taken it through United States territory, and brought much profit to his business interests; but Van Horne, American-born though he was, stood four-square against this. For him it must be an all-Canadian route. He carried the CPR Syndicate with him, and opened up a bitter feud with Jim Hill that lasted a lifetime.

Travelling over the line today it does not need much imagination to picture what the job of building it was like, when the track had to be blasted through a primeval wilderness of rock and muskeg; carved out of vertical walls of solid rock on the edge of Lake Superior, in the depths of winter when the Lake was frozen solid, and all materials for construction had to be brought over the ice; when there was no money left to pay the men's wages. Van Horne was the supreme general. He saw to it that every constructional gang, no matter how severe the weather, how remotely they were located, had ample food. A gourmet himself, his men had the best. He paid them by cheque. There was not the slightest chance of their getting to banks to try and cash them while he and his colleagues in Montreal used every lever they could devise to try and get more funds, so that money would be available when needed. And as we sped on through the rock and muskeg country the mist was lifting, to reveal a brilliant blue sky, and our first sight of Lake Superior was of sparkling waters.

By the time we actually came to the Lake, all traces of the early mist had gone, and I saw it all in ideal conditions. We left Marathon and headed for a solid rock wall, rising sheer from the mirror-like waters of the Lake. I saw the track ahead swinging steeply round to the left and following one of those incredible ledges cut in the very face of the cliff. Red Sucker Tunnel took us through the solid rock of an out-jutting bluff; then came Mink Tunnel. As for Lake Superior itself, it is so vast that looking out over it is just like looking out across the open sea and recall, too, that in winter it is frozen solid! After Mink Tunnel we were running inland for a spell, through wild rocky country, and then at a point about 100 miles from the start of my own cab riding, at White River, we came to Jack Fish Bay. Expressions such as 'horseshoe' when applied to the alignment of a railway are usually picturesque exaggerations of the truth; but there is nothing of this about the Canadian Pacific at Jack Fish. The line encircles on three sides a blue, mirror-like inlet of the sea running for most of the circuit on ledges cut in the 'iron' cliffs descending vertically to the water. It was exciting enough to look back at the 13-car Canadian following behind us on this spectacular location, but imagine what it would be like with a 100-car fast freight! Just after passing through Jack Fish Tunnel my friends in the cab pointed out the cairn erected to commemorate the driving of the last spike to complete the eastern end of the great transcontinental line between Montreal and Winnipeg. This ceremony took place on 16 May 1885, and it marked the end of the greatest anxiety Van Horne had in the entire constructional work. My cab riding covered the Heron Bay subdivision, 118¼ miles in all, and ended at Schreiber. Our average speed had been 40 m.p.h.—remarkable in such a terrain.

A few days later, while in Winnipeg, I had a great treat. It is one thing to read about an epic of railway construction, travel over the line, and let imagination drift back over many decades; but to see some of the locomotives involved—well, in the City of Winnipeg, on a plinth, there is the *Countess of Dufferin*, the first locomotive to have run in Manitoba, built in the USA by Baldwins, and ferried up the Red River by barge. That famous and typical American 4–4–0 which was landed at St Boniface, opposite Winnipeg, in 1877, is now no more than a museum piece; but also in Winnipeg is an even older 4–4–0, built for the Canadian Pacific by Dübs & Company in Glasgow in 1874, and this truly glorious old warrior is still in working order and hauls passenger trains. How this magnificent 'period piece' of a locomotive came to be saved from the scrapheap and preserved in working order is a longer story than can be told here. I can only tell how I was taken to her berth near the Union station of Canadian National; how I met the dedicated and skilled enthusiasts of the Vintage Locomotive Society, and rode on the footplate of the engine over the tracks of that astonishing enterprise, the Prairie Dog Central Railroad. The Society is allowed to operate fare-paying passenger trains over a section of the Cabot subdivision of Canadian National, and the locomotive is old 22 of the Canadian Pacific.

Here indeed I was in the steps of Van Horne, because although the track now so happily titled Prairie Dog Central was not part of the CPR, old 22 is one of a type that could well have been driven by Van Horne when he also was 'out the line'. It was a brilliantly fine Sunday morning and, with a train of three lovely old coaches, described as 'turn of the century wooden, open window, prairie air-conditioned, complete with smoke and cinders,' we made our way cautiously out of the back yard of the Union station and, with bell tolling, steamed out on to the main line west. As yet we had no passengers, but I was thrilled to hear the rich musical tone of the bell, so different from the metallic clanging of the bells on the North American diesels. Riding on the footplate reminded me of many British 4–4–0s, because there were large toolboxes on either side of the cab. On old 22, like those British engines of awkward memory, I sat with my legs hanging uncomfortably down, in the way of the fireman and getting very hot.

We came to a junction, and took the right-hand fork on to the little-used branch line that has become the Prairie Dog Central. There we found our passengers waiting at a little private booking office. I met the rest of the train crew, enthusiastic young people who run the buffet car, the train hostess, and the guard who like the driver was a regular railwayman. So we set off at a gentle speed across the dead level of the prairie track. We were soon away from all dwellings and, with the straight track stretching far ahead, looking through the front cab glass of that old engine, it was not difficult to imagine what things were like when railways were first built across these lands. All too soon we came to the end of the Prairie Dog Central 'concession', an unattended passing loop named Headingley out on the open prairie. The engine was uncoupled, ran round the train, and then took us back to the starting point, running tender first. It was a delightful day, and a memorable weekend interlude between riding the big modern trains.

That same night I boarded The Canadian once more to travel to Calgary, which was reached just after lunch next day. Two new friends were waiting to meet me on the platform, and they gave me a very proper introduction to the place by taking me, within minutes, up to the top of the Husky Tower. This is one of those modern buildings which, like the Post Office Tower in London and the 'Summit' in Sydney, out-scrape the skyscrapers. The Husky Tower in Calgary was built by the Canadian Pacific, and with the trans-continental expresses stopping for half an hour passengers are allowed to break their journey with a lift to the top of the tower, for payment of one dollar. We had plenty of time, and so I was able to drink in details of the amazing panorama at leisure. Inevitably, I suppose, I looked towards the Rockies. A range of foothills prevents their being seen from ground level, but from the tower the entire range was in view—still fifty miles away, but looking superb in their jagged snow-capped array. From the tower the great railway complex of Calgary was spread out like some 00 Gauge model. I watched the train by which I had come leave for the west and the eastbound Canadian approach and stop in the station just beneath. I have, on countless occasions, watched the movement of trains over a wide area on signal box control panels, but this actual viewing surpassed all.

Perhaps not quite all! I was taken to the Control Office in one of the rooms at the base of the Husky Tower from which all the main-line train movements are regulated. The westbound Canadian had not after all passed beyond our ken when we had seen from the top of the tower its rear dome car disappear in the far distance round a curve in the line; for on the centralized control signalling panel its indication lights were coming on and off as it passed over successive track circuits. By that time it was more than sixty miles away, entering the very heart of the mountain country, near Banff, and it was under the scrutiny and safeguards of modern railway operating as surely as when passing just outside a signal box. There undoubtedly was a tremendous spice of adventure when the pioneers of the CPR set out on locomotives like old 22, armed with no greater safeguard than a despatcher's written order, to make their way into the mountains; but there is grandeur no less in the sophistication of modern control, which feeling is emphasized a hundred times when one sees even the great trains of today against the colossal mountain masses west of the 'Great Divide', at the provincial boundary between Alberta and British Columbia.

Even in early autumn, when I was first travelling this way, the westbound Canadian passes through the most exciting scenery in the failing light of early evening, and my own programme was arranged so that I should come eastbound through the mountains by CP Rail. I left Vancouver and slept well through the earlier part of the night, but I had awakened when we had stopped briefly at a small station named Salmon Arm. We were getting near to one of the most historic places in all the world's railways. With Van Horne, the two men who were carrying the immense burden of getting the Canadian Pacific built were George Stephen and Donald A. Smith, both Highland Scots, and once when Stephen was in England trying to raise funds, and things were so bad in Canada that Smith was losing heart, Stephen had wired in the words of the rallying war cry of the Clan Grant 'Stand fast Craigellachie'. This fired Van Horne's imagination, and he determined that when the last spike was driven the place where the act took place should be named Craigellachie. It was on 7 November 1885, and a cairn was erected at the lineside, 28 miles short of the big divisional point of Revelstoke, where at 6 a.m. I was to change over from my sleeping car to the engine cab. In the semi-darkness I did not see the cairn, and I suppose few travellers today know of its existence, still less of its supreme significance. Both the eastbound and westbound Canadians pass it in darkness, and there are no other passenger trains.

We came to Revelstoke that morning in the delicate half-light of a cloudless dawn, and on the platform I met Walter Paffard, Assistant Superintendent of the division, who was going to ride with me through to Field. Revelstoke, set deep in the majestic mountain country west of the main range of the Rockies, is a major locomotive centre. Paffard showed me the workings for the day. He had to provide power for eight eastbound and seven westbound freights, in addition to the two Canadians. These latter each had three locomotives, but those fifteen freights required no fewer than *sixty-three* locomotives between them. We were mounting into the very heart of the Selkirk Range. In the pioneer days no one was certain that there was *any* way through from the west, and when eventually the fiery Rogers found the pass that was named after him the railway location nearing the summit was meandering and on very steep gradients. We neared the station named Glacier, set in an amphitheatre of the greatest mountains I had ever seen. Many of them rise to more than 10,000 ft, and instead of taking the old location which has now been abandoned, we headed straight for Mount Macdonald through which the great Connaught Tunnel goes for five miles in a straight line. This tremendous work, which was opened in 1916, shortened the line between Revelstoke and Beavermouth by 4¼ miles.

Descending from the eastern end of the tunnel at Stoney Creek to Beavermouth, in the Columbia Valley, is one of the greatest obstacles to train operation in the whole world. An incline that requires the use of *thirteen* 3,000-horsepower diesel-electric locomotives strikes one as something very much out of the ordinary. The actual gradient over the 14¾ miles from Beavermouth up to Stoney Creek is not as steep as some of those I have seen elsewhere in the world, in Switzerland, for example, or on the Western Ghats in India. It is what has to be hauled up that makes the problem. The coal trains from the Crowsnest Pass mines to Roberts Bank, near Vancouver, of which there are two a day, are loaded to 105 cars, making a total of 12,400 tons per train, and the locomotives are disposed in three groups: four in tandem at the head end; five, robot-controlled from the head end, somewhere near the middle of the train; and then another four with a second engine crew at the rear. The leading driver thus has nine locomotives, four under his direct control and five under robot control, and all the time he is in radio communication with the rear-end 'pusher' engineman, and with the guard—or conductor, as he is known in North America. When we had made our way gently down the Beaver Hill we found one of the coal trains waiting to go up; but it was one of the smaller standard formation, 88 cars, so it needed *only* eleven locomotives!

At Golden two more enormous freight trains were waiting to move off westward, while we headed eastwards into the narrow gorge of the Kicking Horse Canyon. In this region of overwhelming natural beauty, where early morning mist had now dispersed, and dazzling white mountain peaks were hanging wraith-like across a limpid blue sky, one hardly knows on which to confer the greatest superlatives—the scenery, or the sheer *impressement* of the railway working. All the mountains in this area are named after men famous in the projecting and construction of the Canadian Pacific Railway and, nearing Field, seen to the north, is the entire range named after Van Horne. It would perhaps not be true to suggest that Van Horne built greater than he knew; for, although there is a sensational difference between little 4–4–0 locomotives like that working on the Prairie Dog Central and the teams of diesels that a single engine crew can control now on the mountain grades, Van Horne was a man of immense vision, and everywhere along this magnificent railway one feels as if one is travelling in his footsteps, along his road—as Omer Lavallee has so rightly called it. And so we got away again for the ascent of the Field Hill, up the Kicking Horse Pass to the Great Divide. The gradient here was originally 1 in 22, but since then, following in the Swiss style, two spiral tunnels have been constructed which doubled the distance to be run by the trains and halved the gradient. But Switzerland does not witness what I saw from the lineside on the Field Hill, and which is an everyday occurrence, when the head end of a maximum-tonnage freight emerging from one of the spirals crosses at right angles over its own tail, which is still going in! The remarkable photographs that my friend Eric Johnson took on this occasion provide a more effective epitome of CPR working in the mountains than any words of mine could possibly do.

In Winnipeg I had seen vintage locomotives of the earliest Canadian Pacific days, while at varying stages of my journeys through Canada I had seen, as museum pieces, CPR locomotives of varying ages and sizes. But while I was in Vancouver I was taken to Drake Street depot to see one of the great 'Royal Hudson' 4–6–4s that had been saved from the scrapheap. This class owes its special name to the use of engine No. 2850 for hauling the Royal Train when King George VI and Queen Elizabeth made their great tour of Canada in 1939. The engine I saw at Drake Street had been newly painted and was ready for exhibition. She was not in steam, but I was able to climb on to the footplate, study the controls, and appreciate the colossal size of everything, compared with British and European locomotives. When I saw her thus her eventual destination was uncertain, but since then she has been leased to the British Columbia Railway for the delightful purpose of running steam specials from North Vancouver as far north as Squamish. This line runs along the shores of the very beautiful salt water inlet, Howe Sound. The main line of the British Columbia Railway continues through well-nigh incredible scenery at times, almost to the borders of the Yukon; but the run to Squamish and back makes a splendid excursion from North Vancouver, travelling with such a grand steam locomotive and seeing the rugged fiord scenery of the west coast.

Although most of my activities 'out the line' in Canada were connected with passenger trains, there was one experience with a multi-engined freight that will always live in my memory. In the last chapter I told of blizzard conditions on the Algoma Central and how the freight traffic continued to flow. Two days later, when all that remained of that storm was the immense banks of hard frozen snow ploughed to the lineside, trees weighed down by the weight of the snow and a still thick covering upon frozen lakes and rivers, we were returning from Hawk Junction to Sault Ste Marie with our business car attached to a maximum-tonnage freight, leaving at 4.30 a.m. As a footplate experience it seemed one not to be missed and, in case I overslept, I asked Stan Chapman to give me a call at 4 a.m. It was very cold, with a brilliant moon, and from our car I climbed along *five* locomotives in tandem to reach the leading unit; and I looked ahead along the track where the powerful headlight shone and made the ice and snow sparkle on the cuttings and the trees. Even before we started it was one of the most beautiful sights I have ever seen from a locomotive cab. We had 68 cars behind us—5,000 tons—and even without having to climb gradients like the Beaver Hill, there was much hard work ahead.

One of the great problems on the Algoma Central is the very frequent changes of gradient, and the incidence of severe and continuous curvature. There are not many places where you can settle down to a long hard 'slog'. Very often the locomotives will be climbing a stiff gradient while the tail of the train is running downhill, and with a train of this length there are not many places where you can see the rear vehicles. They are most likely to be out of sight round curves, behind embankments or deep in the woods. The sound of those five diesels going all-out up some of the hardest gradients at about 15 m.p.h. was something to remember, while it was fascinating to see the glistening ice-bound countryside lit up in the engine headlight, as the beam swung from side to side rounding the many curves. It was April, and dawn came before 6 a.m.; it was a cloudless one, and the colouring with the strengthening light was exquisite. After three hours in the cab I began to realize I was getting very hungry, and so I took advantage of slow running through one of the passing loops to climb back along those five locomotives and join my friends in the business car for a hearty breakfast.

Meanwhile the train continued uphill, down across deep ravines, up again, all without any stop till nearing Ogidaki, where we had an order to meet the daily northbound passenger train. We were there first, at 10.03 a.m., and drew slowly to stand in a beautiful situation beside a frozen snow-covered lake. We had run the 117 miles from Hawk Junction in 328 minutes, averaging 21½ m.p.h. While we waited I climbed down from the car to enjoy the mountain air in brilliant sunshine, and to photograph our locomotives. Chatting to our driver again I felt I could not have had a more splendid ride—another memorable experience 'out the line'.

# 15 Electric Scots

In that charming and at times poignant operetta *The Sound of Music* the young heroine sings of her remedy for depression, when all around her seems to be going wrong. I have felt like that many times in my life, and I must admit I have found her remedy a winner every time: 'I simply remember my favourite things, and then I don't feel so bad.' I have many favourite things, far removed from railways; but 'out the line' the sight and sound of West Coast expresses climbing Shap come very near to my 'number one'. The lineside near the Shap Wells intermediate block signals was always one of my favourite haunts. There was an atmosphere there that was difficult to explain. There was not even the accompaniment of magnificent mountain scenery. The line emerges from the northern end of the Lune Gorge at Tebay, and climbs over bleak, windswept moorlands to Shap summit; it was perhaps because it was the culminating point in the London and North Western part of the West Coast main line to Scotland, the ultimate yardstick of engine performance, that it attracted spirits kindred to myself. There was not a very good chance of getting a spectacular smoke effect, because there would be no point in further building up the fire. In a couple of minutes they would be over the top, and coasting or steaming very easily down to Carlisle.

This is not to say engines would not be working hard. One could not take liberties with Shap! Nevertheless, in indulging in a little nostalgia, in remembering some favourite things, one can perhaps appreciate all the better what astonishing changes have come over the scene since 1974. So, let us go back first to 1922 when I took some of my first photographs on the line. The 'ten o'clock' from Euston, the train that five years later was named the Royal Scot, then ran in two sections north of Crewe, the first for Glasgow, and the second for Edinburgh and Aberdeen. I saw it one day in April when it was down to the minimum loading. The first section had six coaches, and the second eight. Both were hauled by LNWR 'Claughton' class engines, and both were climbing very fast, with loud, far-sounding exhausts. Then there was a day of alternating storm and sunshine at Whitsun 1931 when the wind was so strong that Mac Pearson and I were glad to shelter behind the surfaceman's hut at Shap Wells. When the Royal Scot came up the bank the exhaust was being blown horizontally at right angles to the track. They had the normal twelve-coach train of those days and, although on time, were not making much more than 20 m.p.h. Engine and men had worked through from Euston, and by that time they had been on the road for more than five hours and the fireman had probably shovelled the best part of six tons of coal. It was quite typical of 'Royal Scot' engine performance at that time. At Shap Wells they were definitely fighting the gradient.

To the very end of steam days, except with certain trains on which the loads were strictly limited, it was rare to climb Shap without the speed falling considerably below 30 m.p.h. This was little more than fifteen years ago. If an enthusiast and habitué of the lineside at Shap Wells had then gone abroad, and not kept in touch with home railway affairs, it is really difficult to imagine what his reactions would be if he had returned and gone to Shap Wells again, in 1975, to watch the trains. There must be very few places in the world where the speed of passenger trains has *quadrupled* in the last fifteen years, but he would have seen not one or two specially favoured trains, but all the Electric Scots, one after another, coming up the gradient at 85 m.p.h., at the very least. The timetable allowance for the 5½ miles from Tebay up to Shap summit is now uniformly 4 minutes for all the daytime passenger trains. This is an average speed of 82½ m.p.h., and as speed has to be reduced to 80 m.p.h. over the crest of the incline the speed up the main part of the incline must of necessity be much higher than 82½ m.p.h. Often it is near *ninety*. And quite apart from what any lineside observers might think, just imagine what the feelings of an old-time steam driver would be at the idea of having to shut off power to observe a speed limit of 80 m.p.h. over Shap summit!

The speed of the Electric Scots climbing Shap, and equally that on the Beattock Bank, another 75 miles to the north, is the most sensational manifestation of the power of electric traction on the entire main line between London and Glasgow. On the level stretches of line the largest steam locomotives could haul trains of twelve or thirteen coaches at anything up to 85 m.p.h., and the diesels could do 90 or 95 m.p.h.: it is only the alignment of the track, and purely mechanical considerations of design, that hold the blue electric locomotives down to 100 m.p.h. But the 'ton' it is nevertheless, and their tremendous potentialities are held in reserve for the gradients. To stand at the lineside and see them go is itself a never-ending thrill for me. A few years ago I was one of the contributors to a television series called *Steam Horse—Iron Road*, and one of my programmes concerned the building of the early lines. We sought out major feats of civil engineering, and with producer and cameramen based near London one of the sites I chose was Tring Cutting—a colossal feat of manual digging by Robert Stephenson's work force. Our filming included some of the trains, and as, one after another, the blue electrics came streaking up through the cutting, all doing 95 to 100 m.p.h., I was amused to see the cameraman edging further and further back from his original stance close to the line.

We were, indeed, standing beside what is unquestionably the busiest main line in the world. Where else are there flights of six hundred-mile-an-hour trains at six-minute intervals, repeated every hour throughout the day: trains leaving Euston at 40 minutes past every hour, followed at 45, 50 and 55 minutes past, on the hour, and 10 minutes past, and every one going out to do the 'ton'! But even for the most technically minded statistics do not ring the bell quite so thoroughly as the opportunity of seeing it in the flesh. This was very much in my mind in 1969, my year of office as President of the Institution of Railway Signal Engineers. It had become traditional that we had an autumn technical visit, which our Continental members were encouraged to attend; and, while the Saturday occasion was a mammoth affair for the whole membership, we usually contrived to have a little 'special' for the overseas members on the preceding day. In 1969 the main visit was to see the very large new panel signal box at Derby, and on the Friday I felt that the visiting engineers from France, West Germany, Holland, Switzerland and elsewhere should see rather more of our new electric railway than they could by merely travelling to Crewe and inspecting a monster telecommunications centre there, before going by road through the Peak District to Derby. So it was contrived that on the way down to Crewe we should travel by trains that admitted of a pause at Bletchley.

Now Bletchley is not one of the most modern of British signal boxes, albeit one of the panel type, controlling a considerable mileage; but it is without doubt the finest place on the entire West Coast main line for seeing the electric railway at its busiest and fastest. A train running at 100 m.p.h. can be an impressive sight in any locality, but in the confines of a station it can be stunning. Our party had scarcely arrived at Bletchley and was being marshalled ready to walk over to the signal box, when a southbound flyer came through, and before we had reached the box, less than five minutes later, came another, going equally hard. And while those Continental guests of ours listened attentively and appreciatively to the lucid technical explanations given, the atmosphere was enlivened—

whoosh!—by train after train, all sweeping through at much the same speed. The indication lights of their whereabouts, and the closeness of the headway between them, were apparent enough; but time and time again I saw eyes straying from the sophisticated equipment inside the signal box to the vivid reality of the actual trains. There was no doubt they were going!

While the southernmost end of the line is by far the busiest, by day, and Bletchley is not far from its mid-point between London and Rugby, it is in the north country that the most startling manifestations of the Electric Scots are to be seen. The very name Shap seems to have captured the imagination of non-technical writers ever since the days of the first Race to the North in 1888, and some of these writers have got themselves thoroughly mixed up between the climbing speeds on the incline itself and the speeds attained running down from Shap summit to Carlisle. One of the wittiest and most erudite of early railway *littérateurs*, Charles Rous-Marten, once made merry at the expense of a journalist in the *Railway Magazine* as long ago as 1907. He wrote 'I observe that in one of those most extraordinary railway articles which now and then ornament the columns of the halfpenny daily Press, it is stated that during the "Edinburgh race" "Marmion" '—one of the dainty little 7 ft 6 in. single-wheelers of the 'Lady of the Lake' class—'ran from Crewe to Carlisle, over the Shap summit, at a rate of 90 MILES AN HOUR! One cannot of course argue such a preposterous point; one can only exclaim, with Dominie Sampson, "Prodigious".'

'Imagination can sometimes go a long way,' Rous-Marten continued, 'yet it wholly fails to see *Marmion* bucketing up Shap's 1 in 75 at the rate of 90 miles an hour. It is thus that the festive penny-a-liner adds so much to the gaiety of nations!' I may add that, far from running at 90 m.p.h. or anywhere near it on any part of the line, *Marmion* and her kind were not at any time used on the Edinburgh racing train of 1888 on the Crewe–Carlisle section. *Marmion* and *Waverley* shared the running between Euston and Crewe—but not at 90 m.p.h. Some years later the aura of Shap captured another journalist when the LMS accelerated the Royal Scot express to a five-hour non-stop run from Euston to Carlisle, and banner headlines appeared in one newspaper next morning: '79 m.p.h. on Shap Fell.' The actual speed, with the famous Stanier Pacific *The Princess Royal*, was 27¾ m.p.h., and the '79', which was the maximum *downhill* over the entire run from London, occurred nearly 30 miles north of Shap summit on the last miles steeply downhill into Carlisle. Now, in the daytime at any rate, one can really see Anglo-Scottish expresses 'bucketing' up Shap at 90 m.p.h., or very near it. The fastest I have done personally is 88 m.p.h., but my friend Derek

Cross, the distinguished photographer of high-speed trains, has been up at 95 m.p.h.

Nowadays the night hours can be even more impressive. In the aftermath of the Edinburgh race of 1888, the *Pall Mall Gazette* of 6 September carried a very well-informed and comprehensive 'extra' summarizing the progress of the race, and this included the following vividly written paragraph:

> A foreigner taken on to the midnight platform at Shap in the earlier nights of August would have been surprised to see *five* expresses roaring through within two hours, one laden with 'Horses and Carriages only', another full of beds and lucky people whose rest the North-Western will not allow to be broken by the entry of a single passenger between Euston and Perth, all five steaming without a stop the ninety miles from Preston to Carlisle, except one (from Liverpool and Manchester) which takes the 105 from Wigan in a breath.

I wonder what the reaction would be today, from a 'foreigner', a railway enthusiast, or perhaps from one of those persistently ill-informed and soured critics of the railways, if they were taken for a night's vigil at Shap today. True, there is no station platform on which to saunter or munch one's sandwiches; but about the witching hours, say from 00.30 till 02.30, the visitor would see not five expresses, but *fifteen*, and if he stayed for another hour, he would see twelve more! Although not so fast as the day trains, every one of these would be climbing the 5½ miles from Tebay up to Shap summit in 6 minutes. Twenty-seven express trains in three hours: only three are carrying passengers, the Inverness sleeper, the Irish service via Stranraer, and a sleeper from Manchester to Glasgow. Then there is the famous West Coast Postal Special—the fastest train on the line during the night hours—and all the rest are freights, now run just as rapidly as the night passenger trains. The Inverness sleeper, for example, is given 78½ minutes for the 90 miles from Preston to Carlisle; the train only 10 minutes ahead of it is a freightliner of around 1,000 tons from Garston Docks to Glasgow, allowed 82 minutes for the same run. But like my friends from the Continent, who I contrived should see the 100 m.p.h. parade through Bletchley, one needs to see and participate in the extraordinary night procession over Shap to appreciate the full significance of the words 'Electric Scots'.

On a freezing cold winter's night in March 1976 I went out by car from Central Liverpool to Garston Freightliner Terminal. I was anxious to extend my experience of the Electric Scots to the night freight services, and arrangements had been made for me to ride '4S55', one of the heaviest trains on the line. Although the really fast running does not commence until the train is 'under the wires', I determined to see the job from the start, with the train due to leave Garston at 21.42 hours. It was blowing mighty cold as I watched the final stages of loading up. Under the yard floodlights giant travelling cranes moved stealthily up and down, carrying containers to be positioned on the lengthy flat cars. The diesel yard pilot was doing the marshalling, but soon our 'road' locomotive came down out of the darkness, a big 2,750 horsepower Co-Co, of Class '47'. The yardmaster gave us the load, 1,067 tons, almost up to the maximum permitted on this service. Chief Running Inspector John Hughes was coming with me, a very old footplate friend, since I first rode with him when he was firing on the Great Western, at Chester, and we had a splendid run together on the veteran 4–6–0 engine *Saint Vincent*.

No very rapid progress is possible in the early stages of this freightliner run. We had first to get to Edge Hill sidings, on the eastern outskirts of Liverpool, and there 'run round' the train—in other words transfer from front to rear—so that we could proceed eastwards, along the historic route of the Liverpool and Manchester Railway. As we went through the immensely deep Olive Mount cutting, so dramatically pictured in Talbot Bury's famous aquatints of the line in its early days, one could not help wondering what George Stephenson would have thought of the trains of today, and such vast assemblages as ours. Then to Rainhill. Earlier this same day I had breakfasted in Manchester with Michael Satow who built the working replica of *Locomotion* No. 1 of the Stockton and Darlington Railway, steamed so successfully at the time of the 150th anniversary pageant in September 1975. From him I learned that a working replica of the *Rocket* is now projected, ready for running at the time of the 150th anniversary of the Rainhill Trials, in 1979. It is even suggested that replicas—perhaps more reliable than the originals!—might also be made of the *Rocket's* rivals.

While recollections of that pleasant breakfast were still in mind, the big diesel was wheeling our 1,067-ton freightliner along at 62 m.p.h. past St Helens Junction, and we continued at around 60 until coming down dead slow for the sharp curve round on to the West Coast main line at Golborne Junction. Five miles of cautious running, and we drew up on the goods lines within sight of Wigan passenger station, to change engines. We were under the wires in very truth now, and waiting to take us forward were *two* of the latest electric locomotives—ten thousand horsepower between them, and very necessary too. For we had now to run at passenger train speed

—not, it is true, at the breathless pace of the daytime Electric Scots, but fast enough, as I was soon to see. Inspector Hughes and I climbed up into the cab of the leading locomotive. The two were electrically coupled 'in multiple', so that one driver could control the two as a single power unit. A happy bond was immediately established, for our driver, Lawson, of Carlisle, had in his young days fired to Billy Charlton, driver of the 'Royal Scot' class engine *Vesta* on my very first footplate run on a main-line locomotive, as related in Chapter 1 of this book. The span of more than forty years disappeared as Lawson and I talked of steam days 'over Shap'.

In the meantime much was going on around us. Because of traffic delays in the Liverpool area, we were running somewhat behind our normal 'path', having arrived at Wigan at three minutes past midnight, instead of 23.16. Two sleeping car expresses, the first for Inverness and the second for Stranraer Harbour, which we should have preceded, had gone on ahead in their normal path, while another freightliner, the Tartan Arrow company train from Kentish Town to Glasgow, which had been standing on the down relief line, left as soon as the Stranraer was clear. Changing engines on a lengthy freight cannot be done very quickly. Nowadays there is no guard's van at the rear. The guard travels in the rear cab of the locomotive, but before starting he must walk to the rear end to make the brake check. Needless to say these great trains are fitted throughout with the Westinghouse air brake. We were ready to go at 00.26, having cut four minutes from our booked stopping allowance, but we could not immediately pull out on to the main line, because a southbound express freight loaded with huge pipes had to go through first. We got away at 00.30, and although getting green signals at once Lawson was sceptical about our getting a good road. 'The Postal's just behind us,' he said, 'and if she's on time she's already left Warrington.' But the operating that night was superb. The Postal has a ten-minute stop at Preston, and the regulators in the great panel signal boxes at Warrington and Preston judged that if they gave us a run we could be through Preston without delaying the Postal; and so it worked out.

Our own start out of Wigan was simply thrilling. From the station the line climbs the 1 in 104 gradient of the Boars Head Bank and, as Lawson used his 10,000 horsepower to tremendous effect, I thought of Billy Charlton with *Vesta*, back in 1934. He was checked by signal to 20 m.p.h. at the foot of the incline, and with the exhaust roaring fought back to 26 m.p.h. with his 400-ton train. On the freightliner we were doing about 30 m.p.h. through Wigan passenger station, and in those severe $2\frac{1}{4}$ miles, where *Vesta* had toiled back from 20 to 26 m.p.h., we accelerated to 65 m.p.h.; and although it is still uphill after Boars Head, though on easier gradients, we were soon going at the maximum permitted with the freightliners, 75 m.p.h. Downhill towards Preston we continued, doing 72 to 75 m.p.h. all the way, and all signals were green for us to run through the big station, with speed reduced to 25 m.p.h. for the curves at the north end. The time was then 00.46, almost exactly the time the Postal was due, but, although she had much station work to do at Preston, we could not expect to stay in front of her for much longer. She is timed like the daytime Electric Scots.

We ourselves were soon making fast time once again. Over the level stretch towards Lancaster we were doing 75–6 m.p.h. all the way, and coming alongside the M6 motorway for a time north of Garstang we were rapidly overtaking the night juggernauts. It was a calm and fine night, though very cold, with the moon occasionally showing through banks of heavy cloud. The colour-light signals showed up brilliantly, while we passed train after train speeding southwards, passenger and freight alike. The speed had to be eased a little through Lancaster to observe the 70 m.p.h. limit there, but we were soon back at 75 and nearing the shores of Morecambe Bay, at Hest Bank. Then coming into the straight beyond this station we saw ahead what we were expecting—caution signals. We were going into the loop at Carnforth to let the Postal get ahead. We had certainly made good time so far. From passing through Wigan slowly, the next 39¼ miles, to Hest Bank, had taken only 33¾ minutes—just 70 m.p.h. average, and pretty good going with a 1,067-ton freight train. We stopped in the Carnforth loop clear of the main line at 01.13, 2½ minutes before the Postal was due to pass. Cold though it was, I could not resist pushing down the window of the cab to watch for her coming. We did not have to wait long, and then what a spectacle! At 01.17 she tore past, doing by my estimation a full hundred miles per hour.

Perhaps even more impressive was evidence that the signalmen in the panel box at Preston were absolutely on their toes. It is one thing to work smartly when train movements are in progress just outside the cabin windows, as in the old mechanical days. But at Preston the man concerned could rely only on the indications on the illuminated diagram, coming from a junction 27 miles away. But my notes show that no more than *52 seconds* after the Postal had dashed through, the points had been changed, the signal cleared, and we were pulling out on to the main line to chase the Postal all the way to Carlisle. And so effectively did we 'chase' that, not to anticipate anything that happened on the way, she was still in the station when we arrived outside! Between Carnforth and Shap summit there is a vertical rise of 885 ft in 31½ miles of railway, and yet our two electric locomotives lifted that great freightliner train over those miles and up that altitude in 28¼ minutes from the dead start. And from my first timing point out of Carnforth, a miniature summit at the 9½ milepost from Lancaster, our average speed up to Shap summit, 28¼ miles, was 72 m.p.h. In such style are the modern freight trains taken over Shap in the dead of night. On the once-dreaded final 5½ miles up from Tebay, where the gradient is 1 in 75, our two locomotives were for the only time in the journey working anywhere near full power, and we covered that distance in a few seconds under five minutes, with speed falling to 63 m.p.h. near the summit.

Down to Carlisle it was not difficult to run fast. We had to slow down to 20 m.p.h. for civil engineering work on the track between Clifton and Penrith; but we ran freely elsewhere, and I noted one slight excess over our maximum limit speed near Southwaite, 77½ m.p.h. But we were stopped outside Carlisle at 02.14. The Postal was not due away until 02.16 and, although we were not routed into one of the passenger platforms, the shunting pilot was still moving about. We had covered the 62½ miles from Carnforth in 56 minutes, start-to-stop, a truly splendid average of 67 m.p.h., over Shap, and if allowance is made for the long slowing for permanent way work between Clifton and Penrith, the net average speed rises to 69¼ m.p.h. We were kept waiting no more than four minutes outside Carlisle, and stopped on one of the non-passenger lines in the Citadel station at 02.21. Here there was a general changeover. Driver Lawson was relieved. John Hughes made tracks for the up Inverness sleeper, which was already in the station and would take him back to Crewe, while I had a bed waiting for me in the Cumbrian Hotel just outside the station. My notebook contained voluminous notes of a great night's work 'out the line'.

# 16 The Second 'Ton'-K.P.H. Now

Until the year 1973 the fastest I had ever travelled by train was that hectic 114 m.p.h. on the Invitation Run of the Coronation Scot in June 1937. I had several times clocked 100 or slightly over when travelling passenger and once, as told earlier in this book, 103½ m.p.h. from the footplate. But from the mile-a-minute which was the hallmark of an express train in my boyhood, and the eighties and nineties that became commonplace after the Second World War, we are passing well beyond the level hundred. And it so happens, with the change to metrication in Great Britain, that the new prestige speed is going to be 200—two hundred kilometres per hour—with the French moving before very long towards 300. During the past three years I have done some railway travelling at 200 k.p.h. in three countries, much of it in the driver's cab, and my impressions make a vivid contrast to the recollections of my earliest experiences on steam locomotives, now more than forty years ago.

It is not only memories of the footplate that the widening field of travel from boyhood and undergraduate days has left, and it is worthwhile recalling some of the others for the striking comparison they make to my first 'flights' at 200 k.p.h. Using the London and North Western Railway for the greater part of my journeys between Barrow-in-Furness and London, I had come to take it quite for granted that express train travel was quiet, smooth and entirely free from jolts and jars when stopping and starting. Consequently my first journey on the far-famed Cornish Riviera Express was something of a surprise, and I shall never forget the sight of the dining car conductor trying to pour coffee into our cups as we rocketed round curves between Whiteball Tunnel and Exeter. Then I travelled on the 2.15 p.m. Great Central express from Manchester to Marylebone, and the coach in which I rode hunted violently most of the way. As for the Cheltenham Flyer, the locomotive working was always thrilling, but the riding of the coaches was often purgatorial. The celebrated *Punch* cartoonist Fougasse had a splendid drawing of two passengers eating a rather tempestuous dinner, with one saying to the other 'I remember when this train was so horribly slow you could eat your meal in comfort!'

Against all this my earliest impressions of 200 k.p.h. travel are all rather of disbelief. In August 1973 British Railways staged an Invitation Run from King's Cross to Darlington and back with the high-speed diesel train. I was one of their guests on that occasion, and the magnificently straight and almost level stretch between York and Darlington was chosen for a special demonstration of high-speed travel. We ran, very smoothly, at no more than ordinary express train speed as far as York, where we stopped for some additional guests to join. One of these was a retired railwayman who had been prominent in the modernization programme of the late 1950s, and who was architect, from the operating viewpoint, of the big development in marshalling practice with which I had been so closely connected from the engineering angle. He took the vacant seat opposite to me, and we were quickly in animated conversation about old times. I was intrigued at his reaction to the High Speed Train, because north of York we were soon really *going*.

We topped 100 m.p.h. no more than 5 miles out of York, and 200 k.p.h. (125 m.p.h.) just 5 miles farther on. For fifteen miles we made an average of 127¾ m.p.h.—206½ k.p.h.—and so smooth and quiet was the travelling that my table companion just could not believe the speeds I was quoting to him. He said that the running seemed no faster than a normally good run in his time. On this particular stretch that would have meant about 80 to 85 m.p.h. It was, however, on the return journey that an extra spurt was put on. On trials, with only railway staff on board, the train had not long previously made a new British high-speed record, of 141 m.p.h.; and after we passed Northallerton on this trip, doing 128½ m.p.h., still further acceleration began. I clocked one half mile near Thirsk at 138½ m.p.h.—again with the utmost smoothness in riding—but the speed was checked down a little afterwards. In all, the 37¼ miles from Eryholme Junction to Skelton Junction were covered in exactly 18 minutes, an average speed of 124 m.p.h., and we stopped at York to put down those additional guests in no more than 27½ minutes after leaving Darlington, 44.1 miles away. It was a brilliant performance, as much in view of the complete lack of any thrill or sensational experience as in relation to the technical details of the achievement.

A few months earlier I had been in Japan, where almost my first experience 'out the line' was with the New Tokaido line, and its 130 m.p.h. 'bullet' trains. I have used the preposition 'with' rather than 'on' advisedly, because through the courtesy and enthusiasm of my hosts on the Japanese National Railways I had seen the amazing centralized organization in all its ramifications before I had set foot in a single train. In the course of my professional work as a signal engineer, over the years, I have grown up with the gradual development of remote control techniques, from the simple little plants of fifty years ago, in which we worked a single pair of points, or a crossover, and a few signals from a cabin one or two miles away, to great installations like York and Carlisle. But never before had I seen such a place as the central control room at Tokyo. The New Tokaido line running from Tokyo to Osaka, 320 miles, is only the first stage of the nationwide Shinkansen network—the 'new lines'. It was nevertheless a mammoth undertaking, and in this one large room I could see, by indication lights, the train operation on the entire 320 miles of double track.

Now in various parts of the world I have seen some very extensive geographical areas under the control of one modern signal box. In Melbourne, for example, the new standard-gauge line to the Victoria–New South Wales state boundary, at the Murray river, 190 miles of it, is regulated from a single panel in the Victorian Railways headquarters building. In Winnipeg, in one room of the Union station building, three panels control about 1,000 miles of the Canadian National Railways. But these and other remote control plants of varying sizes have a totally different function from that of the Shinkansen line, in Tokyo, on which the traffic operated is at first hearing almost unbelievable. Every fifteen minutes one of the *Hikari* or 'lightning' trains leaves Tokyo for Osaka, while a corresponding procession is travelling northward. These trains make only two intermediate stops, at Nagoya and Kyoto, while a series of slower trains, the *Kodama* or 'echo' trains, runs between the *Hikari* calling at all intermediate stations. At any one time there are about forty trains shown by their indication lights on the large central control panel in Tokyo; and most of these are likely to be travelling at 210 k.p.h.—131 m.p.h.

The first thing that is essential in trying to grasp the significance of this amazing presentation is that the New Tokaido section of the Shinkansen lines is a single purpose railway. There are no trains other than the 130 m.p.h. 'bullets'. When it was first planned there was an intention to run fast freight services at night; but the *Hikari* and their 'echoes' proved so popular that a density of service far greater than anything originally envisaged had to be developed, and a completely clear line during the night hours was essential for track and other maintenance. This makes things simpler from the operating point of view but, with such intense high-speed utilization, the track itself takes a terrific pounding. All the *Hikari* and most of the *Kodama* are anything but lightweight railcar types of unit. The

*Hikari* all consist of sixteen coaches, and the average loading of the entire service, seven days a week, 365 days in the year, is approximately *one thousand* passengers per train. When it is recalled that there is a *Hikari* every fifteen minutes throughout the day, one can calculate that quite a lot of people are being conveyed between Tokyo, Nagoya, Kyoto, and Osaka every day.

In that central control room at Tokyo there are many things beside the big illuminated diagram showing the instant position of every train on the line. Day by day, hour by hour, minute by minute, the running of the trains is monitored on an electrically-operated recording chart. It works automatically, actuated by the passage of trains over the track circuits on the line. The chart on which the record is made has the day's timetable in graphic form printed on it; and as the electrical impulses register the progress of individual trains, the actual times recorded are superimposed upon the scheduled timetable, so that a scrutineer looking at the chart can see at a glance if any train is not running to time. On the day I spent several hours in this fascinating centre everything was 'spot on'. There was the odd minute of variation from schedule, usually a train getting slightly ahead; but nothing to cause a controller to intervene in the virtually automatic operation of the service.

This brings me to another astonishing feature of the line, explained to me in Tokyo, and seen by me from the driver's cab at 130 m.p.h. a few days later. There are *no signals* along the line—and trains are following each other at quarter-hour intervals at 130 m.p.h. Indeed, at those times when a *Kodama* is interposed between two *Hikari*, the interval is considerably less. The traffic regulation is entirely by means of speed indications in the driver's cab of each train. The driver is told at what speed he must drive. Unlike the Victoria Line tube railway in London, the actual driving is not automatic, and if a reduction of speed is required the driver must take immediate action. If he did not do so within a brief interval of time the control of the train would be taken out of his hands. The principle by which this presentation of speed signals in the cab is effected is not new. In the early 1940s there was a freight line of the Pennsylvania Railroad, near Pittsburg, where no wayside signals were used. That great railroad had developed its cab signalling system to a high degree of perfection, in conjunction with a comprehensive system of wayside signalling, and on this purely freight line they tried dispensing with the wayside signals. Like the New Tokaido line it was a single-purpose route.

As the details of the service were explained to me, together with statistics of the number of passengers travelling, I began to wonder how loading up was organized at the terminal stations. Stories that have appeared in numerous articles in the Press of tremendous overcrowding on the Tokyo underground, with men stationed on the platforms to press men and women alike in a solid jam through the doors are not exaggerated. When I found from watching train movement on the illuminated diagram in the Shinkansen Control Centre that the bullet trains were in the terminal stations for no more than 25 minutes, my curiosity was increased. My JNR friends took me to the Shinkansen platforms of Tokyo Central Station for me to see for myself. There, crowd control is one of the most highly organized things I have ever seen. The issuing of tickets is completely computerized, and every seat on the bullet trains can be reserved. A passenger going to the booking office obtains a seat on the first train on which one is available; but if he arrives, for example, about 14.50 hours and the 15.00 and 15.15 are fully booked, he has only to wait till the 15.30 to make his 100 m.p.h. journey to Osaka.

Up on the platforms organization is precision itself. The train due to leave at 15.30, for example, arrives from Osaka at 15.05, fully loaded. No more than five minutes is allowed for all the arriving passengers to clear, and then at 15.10 an army of carriage cleaners goes in. Meanwhile passengers for the 15.30 departure will be forming queues on the platform, at right angles to the line of the rails, precisely opposite the doors of the carriages in which they are reserved. The numbering of the carriages and the door positions are also pinpointed by signs hanging from the platform awning. The cleaners are allowed about a quarter of an hour to do their work, and then no more than five minutes before departure time the passengers pile in—swiftly, efficiently, but with nothing of the 'rugger scrum' tactics that are necessary when loading up the underground trains at the peak of the suburban rush. Then, on the very stroke of time, the bullet train glides out of the station. Five minutes later its place at the platform is taken by the latest arrival from Osaka, and another thousand passengers disgorge into the station concourse.

My first experience of travel on one of the bullet trains was as a passenger. After all I had seen in the central control room and at the depot where the trains are serviced, the first half hour or so was something of an anti-climax. Could we really be doing the 'second ton'? I compared the times I had taken passing the intermediate stations, where the *Kodama* stop, with the mileage; there seemed no doubt that we were cruising at between 120 and 130 m.p.h. Then I began to realize why there was so little sensation of high speed. The Shinkansen is not only a single-purpose railway in respect of its traffic; it is a railway apart from the ordinary walks of life. The old Tokaido line, the first trunk railway in Japan, was built to serve the population and settlements along the route. It followed the east coast, twisting and turning, climbing difficult mountain passes. Speed was of no consideration. On the New Tokaido line, however, speed was everything. It was built on viaducts, over the towns, across tidal estuaries, and where mountains lay in the track it was taken straight through—literally straight. Running thus on an elevated track, with no buildings or natural features adjacent to the lineside, one does not gain any deep impression of exceptional speed, when riding in the comfortable and smooth-running carriages.

One must of course make every allowance for the philosophy of the traveller. Even in countries where railway enthusiasm runs highest, and Japan is not the least of these, one could probably say that 99 per cent of all passengers merely travel to get to the other end. For them a journey that is actually very fast, but almost entirely lacking the sensation of fast travel, is ideal. There is none of the brief thrill of taking off and landing that begins and ends a flight by jetliner. Departure or arrival on the bullet trains is almost imperceptibly gentle. But the connoisseur of railways, whether professional or amateur, is keenly alert to note points; and I must admit that my first impressions, from one of the coaches in the train, were negative rather than positive. It so happened also that the afternoon was hazy and overcast. There was very little colour in the landscape, and the fabulous Mount Fuji, near to which we passed on the way, was no more than vaguely seen. This is rather an extraordinary commentary on what is still the fastest long-distance journey I have ever made by train. For we covered the $213\frac{1}{2}$ miles to our first stop at Nagoya in $120\frac{1}{4}$ minutes, an average from start to stop of $106\frac{3}{4}$ m.p.h.

Two days later I continued to what was then the furthest extent of the line to the south, over the 100 miles from Osaka to Okayama, this time in the driver's cab. From Tokyo to Osaka the train was *Hikari*, but after that it stopped at all stations, four of them in this 100 miles. This new line, like all other extensions to the Shinkansen network, has been designed for a maximum speed of 260 k.p.h. (162 m.p.h.), but at the time I travelled 210 k.p.h. was the maximum actually being run. Speed recording was much easier from the cab than from the carriage, because I could see the kilometre posts, even in the tunnels, where they are illuminated clearly. The acceleration from some of these intermediate stops was tremendous, as from Nishi-Akashi, where we attained the line maximum of 210 k.p.h. in a shade *under* four minutes from rest. The travelling was so smooth, and the line on its viaducts so aloof from the ordinary life of the country and towns, as to minimize the impression of very high speed —more so than when travelling passenger, except when meeting a train going equally fast in the opposite direction. Then there was no doubt about it—we were going *very* fast.

Before I went to Japan I read up all the literature on railways that I could find; and an article in the March 1898 issue of the *Railway Magazine* made me smile when I first read it, and laugh my head off when I re-read it on my return home. 'What should that placid little people know,' the author wrote, 'of the rattle and rush of an express train, typical as it is of the nerve-wasting haste with which we Westerners live our lives?' A little later the writer added 'when Japan finally exchanges her peaceful simplicity, her admiration for and artistic appreciation of nature's beauties, and her contented national life, for the storm, stress and hurry of that feverish existence known to the West, she will have given up the substance for the shadow.'

What would such a writer have had to say about the Shinkansen network? It is, however, not only in the operation of the bullet trains that the Japanese have swept away the 'new and surprising sensation for the jaded globe-trotter' that the writer of 1898 found so attractive, 'that of being absolutely unable to hurry!' I thought of this one day when I was travelling from Takamatsu, on the island of Shikoku, to Shimonoseki in the very far south. Reservations had been made for me on one of the 3 ft 6 in. gauge limited express trains from Okayama, but Tonahara, my guide and philosopher, was concerned to find that the ferry from the mainland was 34 minutes late, owing to fog. There was a short rail journey from the ferry port of Uno up to Okayama, and the connection to the south is a close one without any hazards of late running, and he at once started phoning Tokyo to get me a reservation on a later train. But when the ferry did arrive at Takamatsu there were no freight vehicles to be unloaded and none to be taken on, and we left for Uno only twelve minutes late. Even so it was going to be a very close call at Okayama. To see 1,200 Japanese surging off the ferry at Uno and packing in to the waiting train was the sight of a lifetime—'unable to hurry' indeed!—but this was nothing to what happened at Okayama. As the train neared the station the loudspeakers on our train warned that only three minutes would be available to catch the express for the south; and when 1,200 Japanese are intent upon getting off the platform as quickly as possible, whether they have a connection or not, a past experience of Rugby football is apt to come in useful. How Tonahara and I stormed our way through the crowd, up one staircase, over a long footbridge, down more stairs, just as that imperious bell that heralds the immediate departure of a Japanese train starting ringing, and Tonahara hurled me and my luggage through the first available door with seconds to spare before it closed, is another of those epics that need longer to relate than to experience! To me, who would, I suppose, answer to the name of 'globe-trotter' if not necessarily admit to being a jaded one, changing trains at Okayama did offer 'a new and surprising sensation', but not *quite* in the way that writer of 1898 intended!

The third country in which I have had experience of train travel at 200 k.p.h. is France, and there it has been entirely in the locomotive cab. The former Paris–Orleans Railway, now the South-Western Region of the French National Railways, has magnificently straight and superbly maintained main lines out of Paris. Indeed, the one that leads to Bordeaux and thence to the favoured holiday resorts of the Basque coast, is so favoured as to have a train that averages 90 m.p.h. over the entire 360 miles between Paris and Bordeaux. But the 'Orleans' has its problems in other respects. It was one of the first main lines in France to be electrified, beginning in the 1920s. Train loads were lighter, speeds were not so high, and arrangements for feeding electrical energy to the overhead line were designed to meet the traffic requirements of the day, with a reasonable margin for development. Maximum speeds were then 120 k.p.h. (74½ m.p.h.). Now it takes 2½ to 3 times as much electrical power to run a train of equivalent weight at 120 m.p.h., and so, on a line planned for the speeds of the 1920s and 1930s, you could take, or try to take, more energy from the overhead line than the substations are feeding into it. Consequently, the enterprise of the South-West in putting on very fast train services has to be matched by very careful timetable planning to ensure there is not an undue drain on the electrical supply in the overhead line.

The French Railways kindly favoured me with a cab pass for *Le Capitole du Matin*, the high-speed express leaving Paris for Toulouse at 7.45 a.m. It was a very heavy train, made up entirely of the new *grand confort* coaches. Unlike the British High Speed Trains and the Japanese Shinkansen services, these French 'flyers' are locomotive-hauled, by one of the big 'CC 6500' class electrics, which can exert about 8,000 horsepower. I had become familiar with the working of these locomotives on the line from Paris to Marseilles at speeds up to a maximum of 100 m.p.h., and on *Le Capitole* very high speed did not begin until we had passed Etampes. The curves on the first part of the line preclude anything more than 87 m.p.h. But after we had climbed the gradient to Guillerval, where 'climbing' is really not the appropriate word for a place where we sustained 95 m.p.h., we came out into the open country and, on straight, almost level track, ran continuously at 200 k.p.h.

As in Great Britain, as in Japan, this tremendously fast running was entirely free from sensation or thrill. We were speeding through a wide open countryside, flat in all directions as far as the eye could see. The little country stations flashed by pretty smartly, as did the occasional train in the opposite direction; but the way the senses become so quickly tuned to this fast travelling was revealed when we approached Orleans, and the brakes went on for a careful run through that busy junction. It seemed we were down to no more than walking pace, but when I looked at the speedometer on the dashboard I saw that we were still doing 68 m.p.h. Then away we went for another spell at the 'second ton' onwards to Vierzon. This latter junction marks the end of the very fast running on the Toulouse route, because by then the line is approaching mountain country and the curves in the line preclude anything more than 100 m.p.h. at first, and then 87 m.p.h. Even so, we averaged just over 90 m.p.h. from Paris to our first stop at Limoges, 248¾ miles out.

'Out the line'! What an almost incredible change has come over the whole situation in the past fifty years. I think of the lumbering, hard-riding 4–6–0 on which I made my very first footplate journey, and compare it to the smoothness, quiet, and almost armchair luxury of *Le Capitole* and the Japanese Shinkansen trains. But it is not only a question of bodily comfort, or yet of emotional appeal. When 'out the line' I find myself wearing, at times, so many different hats. As a professional engineer I stand rapt in admiration of what my younger colleagues are now doing, and I am proud to think that the technological advances on British Railways are unsurpassed anywhere in the world. But it is equally true that 'the child is father to the man', and the railway scene that became familiar to me in my later schooldays, and in the years when I was an undergraduate at Imperial College, remains as vividly in mind, and as deep in my railway affections, as the scintillating Electric Scots, the second-ton *Capitole*, and the great centralized-control signalling installations at Carlisle, Munich or Tokyo.

Even among professional engineers I am far from being alone in my addiction to the lore of the older era. Sir William Stanier used to tell a good story about steam and electric locomotives:

> I was in America in 1936 with the Chief Civil Engineer of the LMSR, Mr Wallace. We went to see, on the Pennsylvania Railroad, a method they were using for determining side pressure on rails. We went with the Motive Power Superintendent, Frederick Hankins, and Mr Duer, the Electrical Engineer. It was one of the electrified sections of the Pennsylvania Railroad, and while we were watching this apparatus a number of trains went by hauled by electric locomotives and nobody took any notice. At last a train came by hauled by a 'K 4' 'Pacific', and everybody stopped to look. I said 'There you are, Duer, nobody cares a damn for your tin boxes!'

# Bibliography of works by O. S. Nock


HISTORICAL STUDIES

*Scottish Railways* London, Nelson, 1950
*The Great Western Railway* Cambridge, Heffer, 1951
*The Railway Engineers* London, Batsford, 1955
*Branch Lines* London, Batsford, 1957
*The Great Northern Railway* London, Ian Allan, 1958
*Father of Railways: the Story of George Stephenson* London, Nelson, 1958
*The London & North Western Railway* London, Ian Allan, 1960
*British Steam Railways* London, A. and C. Black, 1961
*The South Eastern & Chatham Railway* London, Ian Allan, 1961
*The Caledonian Railway* London, Ian Allan, 1962
*The Great Western Railway in the Nineteenth Century* London, Ian Allan, 1962
*The Great Western Railway in the Twentieth Century* London, Ian Allan, 1964
*The Highland Railway* London, Ian Allan, 1965
*The London & South Western Railway* London, Ian Allan, 1966
*Steam Railways in Retrospect* London, A. and C. Black, 1966
*History of the Great Western Railway, Vol. 3: 1923–1947* London, Ian Allan, 1967
*North Western: a Saga of the Premier Line of Great Britain 1846–1922* Shepperton, Ian Allan, 1968
*The Lancashire & Yorkshire Railway: a Concise History* Shepperton, Ian Allan, 1969
*Underground Railways of the World* London, A. and C. Black, 1973

BIOGRAPHY

*Sir William Stanier: an Engineering Biography* London, Ian Allan, 1961
*The Railway Enthusiast's Encyclopaedia* London, Hutchinson, 1968

LOCOMOTIVE HISTORY

*Locomotives of Sir Nigel Gresley* (with a foreword by O. V. Bulleid) London, Longmans, 1945
*Kings & Castles of G.W.R.* London, Ian Allan, 1949
*The Premier Line: the Story of London & North Western Locomotives* London, Ian Allan, 1952
*The Locomotives of R. E. L. Maunsell, 1911–1937* Bristol, Everard, 1954
*Locomotives of the North Eastern Railway* London, Ian Allan, 1954

*Steam Locomotive: the Unfinished Story of Steam Locomotives and Steam Locomotive Man on the Railways of Great Britain* London, Allen & Unwin, 1957
*Historical Steam Locomotives* London, A. and C. Black, 1959
*The Midland Compounds* Dawlish, David & Charles, 1964
*The British Steam Railway Locomotive, 1925–1965* London, Ian Allan, 1966
*Southern Steam* Newton Abbot, David & Charles, 1966
*The L.N.W.R. Precursor Family: the Precursors, Experiments, Georges, Princes of the London & North Western Railway* Newton Abbot, David & Charles, 1966
*The G.W.R. Stars, Castles & Kings Part 1, 1906–1930* Newton Abbot, David & Charles, 1967
*The Caledonian Dunalstairs & Associated Classes* Newton Abbot, David & Charles, 1968
*L.N.E.R. Steam* Newton Abbot, David & Charles, 1969
*The G.W.R. Stars, Castles & Kings Part 2, 1930–1965* Newton Abbot, David & Charles, 1971
*G.W.R. Steam* Newton Abbot, David & Charles, 1972
*Engine 6000: the Saga of a Locomotive* Newton Abbot, David & Charles, 1972
*The Gresley 'Pacifics' Part 1, 1922–1935* Newton Abbot, David & Charles, 1973
*The Gresley 'Pacifics' Part 2, 1935–1974* Newton Abbot, David & Charles, 1975

SIGNALLING

*Fifty Years of Railway Signalling* London, Institution of Railway Signal Engineers, 1962
*British Railway Signalling: a Survey of Fifty Years' Progress* London, Allen & Unwin, 1969

HISTORY (SPECIALIZED)

*The Railway Race to the North* London, Ian Allan, 1959
*Historic Railway Disasters* London, Ian Allan, 1966
*British Railways at War, 1939–1945* Shepperton, Ian Allan, 1971
*Speed Records on Britain's Railways: a Chronicle of the Steam Era* Newton Abbot, David & Charles, 1971

LOCOMOTIVE WORKING

*British Locomotives at Work* London, Greenlake, 1947
*British Locomotives from the Footplate* London, Ian Allan, 1950
*Four Thousand Miles on the Footplate* London, Ian Allan, 1952
*Fifty Years of Western Express Running* Bristol, Everard, 1954
*British Steam Locomotives at Work* London, Allen & Unwin, 1967
*Rail, Steam and Speed* London, Allen & Unwin, 1970
*Sixty Years of Western Express Running* Shepperton, Ian Allan, 1973

GENERAL

*Railways of Britain—Past and Present* London, Batsford, 1947
*The Boy's Book of British Railways* London, Ian Allan, 1951
*British Trains, Past and Present* London, Batsford, 1951
*Main Lines across the Border* London, Nelson, 1960
*British Steam Locomotives* London, Blandford, 1964
*Steam Railways of Britain in Colour* London, Blandford, 1967
*Railways at the Turn of the Century, 1895–1905* London, Blandford, 1969
*Railways at the Zenith of Steam, 1920–1940* London, Blandford, 1970
*Railways in the Years of Pre-Eminence, 1905–1919* London, Blandford, 1971
*The Dawn of World Railways, 1800–1850* London, Blandford, 1972
*The Golden Age of Steam: a Critical and Nostalgic Memory of the Last Twenty Years before Grouping on the Railways of Great Britain* London, A. and C. Black, 1973
*Railways in the Formative Years, 1851–1895* London, Blandford, 1973
*The Majesty of British Steam* (paintings by G. F. Heiron) London, Ian Allan, 1973
*Railways in the Transition from Steam, 1940–1965* London, Blandford, 1974
*The Railway Picture Book* (paintings by Jack Hill) London, A. and C. Black, 1975
*Pre-Grouping Scene (G.W.R.)* Shepperton, Ian Allan, 1975
*In the Modern Age* London, Blandford, 1975
*Railways Then and Now: a World History* London, Elek, 1975

OVERSEAS RAILWAYS

*Continental Main Lines: Today and Yesterday* London, Allen & Unwin, 1963
*Railway Holiday in Austria* Dawlish, David & Charles, 1965
*Single Line Railways* (for United Kingdom Railway Advisory Service) Newton Abbot, David & Charles, 1966
*Railways of Australia* London, A. and C. Black, 1971
*Railways of Southern Africa* London, A. and C. Black, 1971
*Railways of Canada* London, A. and C. Black, 1973
*The Algoma Central Railway* London, A. and C. Black, 1975

BRITISH RAILWAYS, OPERATING

*British Railways in Action* London, Nelson, 1956
*British Railways in Transition* London, Nelson, 1963
*Britain's New Railway: Electrification of the London–Midland Main Lines from Euston, Birmingham, Stoke-on-Trent, Crewe, Liverpool and Manchester* London, Ian Allan, 1965
*Electric Euston to Glasgow* London, Ian Allan, 1974

# Index